D. Martyn Lloyd-Jones
HEALING
and the
SCRIPTURES

Those who know Dr. Lloyd-Jones only as an expositor will be delighted to meet him in this book and discover that he was also a gifted counselor and brilliant diagnostician. Anyone who must deal with the personal problems of life, and especially sickness, will benefit from his insights and wisdom. I especially commend this book to pastors who must minister daily to hurting people.

—Warren W. Wiersbe
General Director,
Back to the Bible

Dr. Martyn Lloyd-Jones was a brilliant physician as well as an outstanding preacher, and there is great medical wisdom, as well as deep spiritual and pastoral insight, in these thought-provoking chapters. Here is a masterful view of the Christian physician's calling, and of the dimensions of ministry to the whole man.

—J. I. Packer
Professor of Historical
and Systematic Theology,
Regent College

D. Martyn Lloyd-Jones
HEALING
and the
SCRIPTURES

A Division of Thomas Nelson Publishers
Nashville

Published in Nashville, Tennessee, by Oliver-Nelson Books, a division of Thomas Nelson, Inc., Publishers, and distributed in Canada by Lawson Falle, Ltd., Cambridge, Ontario.

Scripture quotations are from the Authorized Version, Crown copyright.

Chapters 1–8, the appendix, notes and selective bibliography were originally published in 1982 under the title *The Doctor Himself and the Human Condition* by Christian Medical Fellowship Publications, London, England. Second edition published in 1987 under the title *Healing and Medicine* by Kingsway Publications Ltd., East Sussex, England.

Printed in the United States.

Library of Congress Cataloging-in-Publication Data

Lloyd-Jones, David Martyn.
  Healing and the Scriptures.

  Previously published as: Healing and medicine. 1987.
  Bibliography: p.
  1. Medicine—Religious aspects—Christianity.
2. Spiritual healing. I. Title.
BT732.2.L58 1988   615.8'52   87–31244
ISBN 0-8407-9011-2 hc
ISBN 0-8407-9582-3 pb

1 2 3 4 5 6 — 92 91 90 89 88

Contents

To the American Reader

Dr. Martyn Lloyd-Jones was known to many as the prince of preachers. Many a pastor and Bible teacher sat and listened to this master pulpiteer, not only to gain insight from his teaching of the Word but also to benefit from the entire communication process as Dr. Lloyd-Jones "ministered to his congregation."

To many, he was known as the Doctor, an affectionate term that sprang from his serial callings as a medical doctor and then as a preacher. His authority with his subject, *Healing and the Scriptures*, is backed by personal medical expertise as well as scriptural knowledge.

It may be helpful to American readers to understand that in the United Kingdom there is a National Health Service, which offers medical care to all, rich or poor. One's ability to pay has no significant relationship to the type of care offered or the quality of care available. When drugs are needed, a small fee is charged to cover basic costs.

Because of the universality of this health care system—and unlike private care in the United States—patients do not have the privilege of electing which physician will care for them. Rather, patients are examined and cared for by the physician who is on duty at the time.

Dr. Lloyd-Jones held that the changes accompanying the National Health Service—such as payment for services or doctor-patient relationships—should not significantly affect the professional commitment of Christian physicians. These same changes, however, prompted his argument that the church is not only relevant but necessary to the healing process in modern medicine.

Healing and the Scriptures was originally published in Great Britain under the title *Healing and Medicine*.

Introduction

The following pages present typical passages from the papers and addresses given to medical practitioners and students by David Martyn Lloyd-Jones.* Widely—internationally—known from his thirty years of authoritative preaching in the pulpit of Westminster Chapel, London, he had entered the Christian ministry from the medical profession. He left medicine in 1927, on the threshold of what held the promise of a distinguished career as a consultant physician, and throughout his life he remained deeply attached to the profession. He kept his interest in medical research and continued regularly to read the chief medical journals and literature. He changed

*The Rev. David Martyn Lloyd-Jones (1899–1981), M.B., B.S. (1921), M.D. (1923), M.R.C.P. (1925). Formerly Chief Clinical Assistant to the Medical Unit, St. Bartholomew's Hospital, London. Minister of Sandfields Presbyterian Church, Aberavon (1927–1938); Minister, Westminster Chapel, London (1938–1968).

course only because of what were for him the overriding
claims of the ministry.

Dr. Lloyd-Jones' main strength lay in his penetrating grasp
of the Bible's central message and his ability to apply it accurately to the contemporary situation. When in the pulpit his
alert mind was wholly devoted to conveying to the audience
the precise meaning of the text *in its context*. His teaching
ability was such that illustrations were few for he felt little
need to supplement the Bible's material from the best secular literature or anecdote, with the result that few who heard
him could easily forget his text and its essential thrust *in its
original setting*. A now prominent Australian surgeon, who
regularly attended Westminster Chapel during his postgrad-
uate years in London, later commented—"I have always felt
that I there received a complete course in biblical theology
and have greatly benefited ever since."

Out of the pulpit, Dr. Lloyd-Jones made his beneficent influence felt in a number of directions. Chief of these, perhaps, was his impact on the University Christian Unions and
members of the various professions. He gave much of his free
time to the needs of theological students and younger ministers, and also, in their turn, to medical students and junior
doctors. Being deeply read in theology and church history his
accurately discriminating mind was at its best when sorting
out the theoretical and practical problems of ordinands or
busy ministers. One example, which is available in print,
may be seen in the devastating reply[1] to Dr. William Sargant's
book—*The Battle for the Mind* (Heinemann, 1957). This *tour
de force* was given at a ministers' conference and led to an
illuminating discussion. From 1939 to the end of his ministry, Dr. Lloyd-Jones gave up a whole day every month, except
in the summer vacation, to what grew into a largely attended
ministers' conference. Each autumn he also chaired the annual conference for study and discussion of the writings of
the Puritans. His own papers at this conference and sum-

ming up at the end of the day's proceedings were outstanding.

In spite of demands from his own church, and mid-week journeys across the country to bring encouragement to other congregations (and especially to preach at the induction of new ministers to their first charges), he rarely refused aid to the Christian Medical Fellowship. For over fifteen years he chaired the CMF's (London) Medical Study Group at which his restless research mind was given full rein in dismissing inadequately confirmed "findings" or in demanding primary sources for statements which might prove only to rest on popular impression or statements copied from textbook to textbook. Again, his own summing up at each stage of the Group's progress—or, equally, at points of failure to achieve any—were frequently brilliant. The addresses which he gave at the Christian Medical Fellowship's Annual Breakfasts during the BMA meetings at Cardiff 1953, Brighton 1956 and Swansea 1965 were by common consent among the best in a long series of such occasions.

Cold print is a poor substitute for the actual presence of this remarkable personality's convincing tones and incisive reasoning, not to speak of his skillful use of both hands when driving home the truth. Because, in print, each arresting passage often proves so much a part of the warp and woof of a unified total argument, selection has proved difficult. It is hoped, however, that what is most relevant to the contemporary situation has been included.

Dr. Douglas Johnson

CHAPTER 1

The Doctor Himself

I have found myself to some extent in difficulty when determining the subject on which I should speak to you. In the end, I have been governed by a medical dictum. It is a principle of which I am sure you all approve and to which you adhere in your own work. The rule for our action must always be that which is best for the *patient*. I am therefore going to speak about the *doctor himself*. I still know enough about the medical profession to be aware that the men belonging to it have certain particular temptations.

If I were asked to mention the most serious of these I would say that it is a proneness to objectify everything, or in other words, to take a "detached view." I suppose that this is to some extent inevitable. If a medical man were continually to allow himself to be affected emotionally by every case he meets, it is fairly clear that he could not continue long in practice. Breakdown would be inevitable. He therefore has to

Part of an address given at the Annual Breakfast of the Christian Medical Fellowship on July 15, 1953, during the Annual Meeting of the British Medical Association at Cardiff.

put up something of a protective barrier. He must not feel anything too deeply. He must protect himself and his own sensitivity against the assaults which are constantly made upon him by the troubles and worries of others—especially, perhaps, by the fact of death. While that is all perfectly understandable, it does however lead to a particular danger. It becomes a fixed habit of mind. The doctor has so objectified himself that he never faces up to himself and to his own life at all.

Somewhere in Pembrokeshire a tombstone is said to bear the inscription: "John Jones, born a man, died a grocer." There are many whom I have had the privilege of meeting whose tombstone might well bear the grim epitaph: " . . . born a man, died a doctor"! The greatest danger which confronts the medical man is that he may become lost in his profession. Believing, therefore, as I do, that this is the special temptation of the doctor, I should like to call your attention to the parable of the rich farmer in Luke 12:13–21.

In this parable our Lord is depicting a man who prided himself on his worldly wisdom. He looked ahead. He was not one of those men who is easily carried away by his emotions. He was hardheaded, one who took the objective view of everything. He was also a man who was particularly proud of his foresight and the long view which he took of life. He had earlier made such perfect provision that at last the day had come when he was able to congratulate himself. All was well. The great day of retirement had arrived and he was looking forward to tremendous enjoyment of his new leisure. He was that sort of man. What, however, our Lord had to say about him was that he was *a fool*. This description may seem rather harsh and uncalled for. At first it sounds rather cruel. Yet our Lord justified what he said about this man most amply. He was a tragic figure, because he failed just at the point where he had always thought he was strongest. He goes down

14

first in that very point where he thought that he was superior to other people. Of what can we convict him?

He was obviously someone who had never really thought clearly. He imagined that he had. He was of the opinion that he had worked out everything and considered every eventuality. Our Lord saw very plainly that he had not. His thinking up to a point was very fine, very sound, very clear, but the tragedy was that he stopped thinking at a most vital point. He had not catered for the fact of death. He had worked out a program for the whole of his life and then made this fatal assumption that it would go on endlessly.

It is surely one of the most astonishing things about life that we all of us tend to fail to see the things that are most immediately before us. I suggest that this is one of the most remarkable things about the average medical man. He is face to face with the fact of death more frequently than anybody else. But does he see it? Does he apply the fact to himself and to his daily life? It is precisely at this point that objectifying everything exerts its baneful influence. This habit which we unconsciously develop prevents our facing what is so obviously confronting us. We never even give it a thought. I am suggesting that a man who fails at that point really does deserve the epithet that our Lord applied to the man in his parable. He is a fool! I am, of course, fully aware that the average medical practitioner is a sensible man, a hardheaded man and a man of the world. Whatever others may do, he does not take things as they appear to be. Yet there he is, I could say perhaps more frequently than one of any other profession or any other class, failing to see the one thing that is all the time staring him in the face.

You may reply: "We are not interested in death! We are interested in life and health." Yes, but wait a minute! I listened last December to a series of lectures by a doyen of the medical profession. As he looked back across fifty years of medicine there were three things of which he was particularly proud, and where he felt he had really achieved something. The first was eugenics, the second was the antinoise campaign and the third was the Cremation Society. Of course, I suppose, a doyen of the medical profession is entitled to say that those three things are the most important in life! He would justify his interest in terms of what happens to an individual before he is born; his avoidance of noise when he is in this world; and the way in which his corpse is dealt with after he has gone. They certainly do make a big difference to a man's life in this world.

I would, however, apply this identical argument in the very same way. Is there anything that tends to affect life more than death? The fear of death, the assaults which the fact of death makes upon a man's life and upon his whole family relationships? Death, whether we like to admit it or not, is one of the most potent factors in life. Whatever your personal attitude towards this matter may be, it is surely indefensible to refuse to face this inexorable, inevitable fact of death. I ask, do you really face it? Do you go beyond that and ask, what is the purpose of it all, what is it leading to, what lies beyond it? What provision are you making? Our Lord taught that anyone who does not approach along those lines is a fool.

The second count which our Lord brings against this man is that he also has such a poor and unworthy concept of himself. Look at him—his barns are bursting with grain, they have become too small to take in all the wonderful produce of the estate and the sum total of all that he has collected. He now turns to himself and addresses his soul and says—"Soul, thou hast much goods laid up for many years; take thine ease, eat, drink, and be merry." He congratulates himself. We should take special note of the fact that he is talking about his soul. What is his conception of his soul? His concept of the essentials of life seems to have consisted in the aggregate of the things which he possessed. As a man, I protest against

16

such a view of what constitutes a man. Yet is not this view something which is all too common? I suggest that it is the major tragedy of life today. Men have lost the true concept of what a living man is, and have taken to thinking of themselves in terms of possessions and success. Need I further emphasize the matter? You are all perfectly familiar with it.

What is success? It is getting on, building up a reputation. There is nothing wrong in that of itself, but if you make it the main thing in life it is a tragedy. Making money, having a still bigger and better car, getting this honor and that honor and gaining this or that social position may be all right in themselves; but surely a man has lost himself if that is his final estimate of his personality. Is that life? Is that real being? A man who is guilty of such an estimate is really debasing himself. Man is a creature who has been made in the image and likeness of God. He is not a mere reasoning animal. He is not a mere brain or intellectual apparatus. He is a being who was created for fellowship and communion with God. He is intended to be the lord of creation, bearing within him something which is imperishable. He is being meant for and destined for God.

My next count against this man is that, with all his wisdom, foresight and self-protection, he had really made no provision for the future. So when the call came—and you are all able to reconstruct the symptoms and the unexpectedness of his angina, coming as it so often does upon someone who has never felt so fit in his life—he was on top of the world. Then suddenly came that fatal stab. The poor fool, who had prided himself on all the things he had done and the wealth he had amassed, found himself empty indeed. He was then compelled to take that great and long journey from which man never returns. He had made no preparation for it at all.

It is appointed that man must die and after death comes the judgement. Of one thing we can be sure, this tribunal will not prove just to be a postmortem on *what a man has*

17

left behind. It is an examination of what use he has made of the gifts which have been given by God. There is not a man among us but is responsible for the gifts which he has. God intends that all these gifts should be used to his glory. We shall be judged in terms of what we have done with the gifts he has entrusted to us. What use have I made of them? A man who is not prepared for such questions is a fool.

The final point in the story, which calls for notice, is that this man was such a poor judge of riches. He thought of riches purely in terms of material possessions. Yet, surely, our true riches consist in peace of conscience. A man who has ever faced his own conscience would gladly give the whole world for real peace of conscience. How can a man silence this inward voice? How can you comfort yourself when you know that you have done things which are so terribly wrong and when you know that God is eventually to look into them?

How can a man find peace? It is in the gospel of Christ. Here are the true riches—to feel that your life in this world has a purpose and that it is not merely "to get on." It is the antechamber of eternal life. It is the knowledge that death is not the end, but that it will just lead on to the vision of God. Let each think this out for himself. The riches that God offers are made very plain in the New Testament and they need not be left behind when you die. They are most with you and are your comfort in death, when everything else has gone wrong. The true riches are God's gift of "a lively hope by the resurrection of Jesus Christ from the dead," leading "to an inheritance incorruptible, and undefiled, and that fadeth not away, reserved in heaven for you who are kept by the power of God" (1 Pet. 1:3–5).

I seriously suggest to you that these are the things on which every doctor should reflect. On the present occasion you are met in order to consider the patient, his needs, his diseases, the problems and the cures. I have tried to counsel you as a one-time medical man and one who still loves the profession and the men and women who belong to it. I beseech you not to allow the profession to make you forget yourself, that you are a man, and not merely a doctor.

CHAPTER 2

The Supernatural in Medicine

Christian doctors are constantly questioned about this matter, whether by a patient or a relative or some interested person. Someone is desperately ill and medical science, or art as you may like to call it, has done its utmost, but the patient is getting worse and someone suggests the possibility of "faith healing." So the Christian practitioner is confronted with the problem and forced to make a decision about it.

Current interest in America

What really has crystallized the matter as far as I am concerned personally was an experience I had in America two years ago. I was there for about five months. I was asked by certain members of the faculty of a well known theological seminary, at which they tend to be intellectual and sceptical of anything approaching enthusiasm, what I thought of "faith healing," and, in particular, the activities of a lady by

An address to the Annual Conference of the Christian Medical Fellowship at Bournemouth, May 1971.

the name of Kathryn Kuhlman. As it happened I had read the book by her, which bears the title *I Believe in Miracles*;[1] but I was interested to know why they were concerned about this subject. The answer I received was that a well known American preacher had invited Mrs. Kathryn Kuhlman to take meetings in his church. As the result of the fact that it was he who had invited the lady, a certain undergraduate had gone with a friend to the meeting. They had arrived in a very critical mood, but they had come away enthusiastic and greatly impressed, and had written home about their impressions. So the problem had arisen for my friends in a very direct manner. There was much discussion going on about the subject and they wished to learn—how did we assess it? What did we make of it?

Two chief attitudes

I believe I am right in saying that there are two main positions among Christian people with regard to this subject of "faith healing." The first consists of those who are overimpressed by the occurrence of certain phenomena. I put it in that way quite deliberately.

This attitude is manifesting itself in another way in connection with the new charismatic movement. It is also showing itself in unexpected places. The Roman Catholics are becoming involved in this movement, particularly in the United States and in Central and South America. A book has been published called *Catholic Pentecostalism* (Darton, Longman & Todd, 1977). This is a book that is going to compel us to think again and to think very urgently about these matters. There is a very dangerous element in all this for the reason that the main thesis seems to be that theology does not matter. What really matters, they say, is that one has had a living experience of the Spirit which manifests itself in particular gifts. So you can more or less believe anything you like as long as you have these manifestations. I put all this under the general heading of "capitulation to phenomena." It is the position in which your theology and your doctrine are more or less to be determined by phenomena. Those who take this attitude constitute one big group.

The other group consists of those who tend to reject the whole of this *in toto*. They feel that the subject really does not merit much discussion, that we have been hearing about it throughout the years and that the less we have to do with it the better.

Rejection of the claims

I want to examine these two positions and we will start with the second. Those who reject the whole claim for these phenomena—miraculous healing, demonology and speaking in tongues, etc.—do so, I find on the whole, for three main reasons. The first is not so much a reason as a statement of fact. They just refuse to consider the subject at all. The entire concept is dismissed as being psychological or something, perhaps, even worse; but generally psychological. This attitude is based on the consideration of the kind of people who are generally involved in this kind of thing.

With regard to the much publicized happenings at Lourdes among the Roman Catholics, they will not consider any possibility of facts at all. Why? Because of the very origin of Lourdes. It arose from the experience of the simple peasant girl who claimed to have had a vision of the Virgin Mary. There is no need to go any further, they say, there is nothing in it, the whole thing is bogus. Though great claims may be made, they cannot be true. It is impossible by definition, and you should just dismiss it on these general grounds.

Then there are others who reject it all on what they would call scientific grounds. They maintain that the law of nature make such happenings quite impossible, that nature is a closed system and is a matter of cause and effect. Because of this, miracles are impossible.

23

There is yet a third group which I put under the heading of "biblical." This group consists of those who pay very little attention, if any, to all these claims because they hold dogmatically the view that the miraculous and all such spiritual manifestations ended with the apostles and that once we were given the completed canon of the New Testament all such unusual phenomena came to an end. This has been a very common view.

The apparent facts

Those are some of the ways in which people have rejected the very possibility of miraculous healing at the present time. As we review them it seems clear that, first of all, we must face the question of facts. It is surely unscientific to reject facts; and it is no part of our business as Christians to do so. There has clearly been a tendency to be ready to do so. Take the case of Kathryn Kuhlman. She has been the minister of a Baptist Church in Pittsburgh, Pennsylvania, I believe, for over twenty years. She is very well known both to ministers in that city and also to medical men, some of whom are elders in famous churches. These are not wild enthusiasts but balanced, sane men. They do not belong to some strange or wild sect, but are good commonsense Presbyterian elders! Yet these men are prepared to say openly that they can attest the claims that people with organic diseases, in their knowledge, have been cured, and that it is this knowledge that has won them over to support Dr. Kathryn Kuhlman's work. In her second book *God Can Do It Again*,[2] there are cases of healing which are certified by medical men, whose names, medical qualifications and hospital posts are duly reported. Indeed, in one or two of the cases, the medical men themselves were the subjects of healing.

With regard to these witnesses I frankly am in this position. I cannot say that they are liars, neither can I believe that they are deluded. Everything that one knows about these people, or can discover about them, suggests that they are reliable witnesses, and that they have no reason for reporting these facts, or supporting them, save that they believe them to be facts and that they feel in honor and duty bound to say so.

But, for myself, the thing that has impressed me most throughout the years was a little book that I read a number of years ago by Alexis Carrel, whose name is familiar in connection with the Carrel-Dakin solution, which was used in surgical treatment of cuts and wounds immediately after the first World War. He also wrote a well known book called *The Phenomenon of Man*. Now Alexis Carrel wrote a little booklet on the subject of miraculous healing in which he gives an account of something that happened in his own experience. He was a Roman Catholic, but not a practicing one. However, he had become interested in Lourdes and its claims and had decided to go and to investigate it for himself.

In this booklet he gives an account of how he travelled on the train to Lourdes and how he examined there a case of miliary tuberculosis. It had started as intestinal tuberculosis, but it had now reached this terminal stage. He described the distended abdomen and so on. He examined the patient on the train and felt that the patient was *in extremis*. He was doubtful whether the patient would even reach Lourdes alive. However, the next day he saw with his own eyes the cure of this person. He saw the distended abdomen gradually subsiding; and he was able to examine the patient subsequently and could find no evidence of any disease whatsoever. He then went to the Medical Bureau which they have at Lourdes, equipped with X-rays and everything that can be desired. So, without coming to any conclusion as to an explanation, he has just stated the facts.

Changing attitudes of scientists

But still more interesting, it seems to me, is the extraordinary change that has been taking place in the realm of scientific thinking in these last years. Few things in the world of

25

thought are more interesting and more important than this. I do not pretend to understand it all, but I understand enough to be able to follow the argument. The scientific view of the nineteenth century has been abandoned. The controlling theory was deterministic, mechanistic and static in its outlook. It had originated with Descartes and Isaac Newton. They were the fathers of this view and it was universally adopted. Most of us belonging to the evangelical tradition had virtually accepted it and believed that this was the only truly scientific attitude.

The fact is that, as the result of the work of Einstein and others, the theory of relativity and the quantum theory and so on, there is today an entirely new approach. Scientists, the best scientists, are now saying that our knowledge of "the laws of nature," so called, is very limited. What we have called "laws of nature" only describe a part of actuality and of the totality of phenomena. As far as they go they are correct, but all they do is to describe certain common patterns. It is not that the scientists are disputing the existence of these patterns or denying that within the realm of these patterns you can still talk of cause and effect; but what they have discovered is that there are other factors outside these patterns which cannot be explained in terms of our established, or recognized, "laws of nature."

The modern idea is that of "indeterminacy." They talk now about "probability," not certainty. There is a new kind of openness. I was reading an article recently in which the writer did not hesitate to introduce the idea that "the laws of nature," as we call them, may actually be changing, that the rate at which light travels is changing, and the rate at which certain other phenomena come to pass is changing. So that, with this new view of science, it is no longer taught so confidently that "the laws of nature" govern events. The new view of energy, and especially electrical energy, is such that you must only talk about "probabilities." There are all sorts of possibilities, and we have no right to be dogmatic and to lay down as a rigid principle that you will always have cause and effect.

This new attitude can be worked out, of course, in many ways. The change is most encouraging because, among other things, the holding of the older concept meant that, in the end, there was no purpose in holding any view whatsoever, because even one's thinking was the result of some predetermined cause leading to an effect. The whole process was mechanistic and what a man happened to believe was regarded as the result of forces outside his own control. There was no volition and no such thing as action; and ultimately, of course, it led to the exclusion even of God. If nature is a closed system, then there is no need of God, indeed no room for God, and most scientists did not believe in God at all. However, we are concerned about this great change in scientific thinking more as it affects our particular subject.

Exaggeration of biblical claims

Then, when you come to the rejection of these facts and phenomena in terms of supposed biblical teaching, I personally have always found myself quite unable to accept the well known teaching that everything belonging to the realm of the miraculous and the supernatural as manifested in New Testament times came to an end with the apostolic age. There is no statement in the Scripture which says that— none at all. There is no specific or even indirect statement to that effect.

Likewise, I am not satisfied by B. B. Warfield's answer to those who have claimed that miracles did continue after the apostolic age.[3] It is well known that Tertullian and Augustine both made use of the argument that miracles were happening in their time and age in defense of, and as a part of their apologetic for, the Christian faith; and I have never been satisfied with Warfield's answer to that. Even among themselves scholars are not agreed that you can dismiss the evidence in that summary manner. Not only that, but as one who has been very interested in the history of the Scottish Covenanters and the early Scottish reformers, I have always been impressed by evidence that comes from those times. There are incidents reported in the life of John Welch, the son-in-law of John Knox, where it seems clear that miracles were performed in certain strange and extreme circumstances. There is the famous Covenanter, Alexander Peden. It seems to me to be beyond any dispute that that man had the power of foreknowledge and did prophesy things that subsequently came to pass. The records are authentic and they can be read in the two great volumes of *Select Biographies* edited for the Woodrow Society that deals with that kind of history.

Periodicity in the Bible

Furthermore, I would suggest that in the Bible itself there is surely discernible a kind of periodicity in the appearance of these supernatural happenings. For instance, there is clearly a periodicity in the Old Testament. These things happened at special given times, and for clear and obvious reasons. The same is seen in a measure in the New Testament; and we are told that the Spirit is the Lord of these matters and dispenses his gifts according to his own will. This is something therefore that can happen at any time when it is the will of God that it should happen. Who are we to determine when this should be?

It seems quite clear that, taking the Christian era in general, there was a profusion in the number of such events at the very beginning which has not continued. As I have said, I am not satisfied that they have never happened since, but, speaking generally, they have tended not to happen. During those great periods of revival which have come periodically in the history of the church, the phenomena consisted not so much in the working of miracles or healings as in extraordinary power of preaching and extraordinary depth of conviction, and an unusual element of joy and exultation. All that, it seems to me, is within the lordship of the Spirit. The fact that this has generally been the story in our Christian era is no proof that at any given point there may not be a reintroduction of other kinds of phenomena and especially as we approach the end of the age. In addition to this, those who have been interested in reading books like, for instance, *Pastor Hsi of China*, will have come across incidents and events which I, at any rate, could not explain except in terms of the supernatural and the miraculous. It seems as if God has granted them in the initial stages of a given work, or when some special attestation of the truth has been needed.

Changing attitudes in medicine

More positively, I believe there are certain other facts to which we have not given the weight and attention that they deserve. There are certain medical facts, it seems to me, that we have tended to discount. I am referring to the reports of spontaneous cures, and particularly regressions in the case of cancerous growths. I had the pleasure of meeting in Cincinnati a man engaged in medical research. He had been working in Chicago with two others who had collected 244 cases of spontaneous cures of cancer in the medical literature in the United States. He was able to show me one of their articles in which this was reported. I remember how when a number of us were looking into this matter under the auspices of the Christian Medical Fellowship we came across several examples in medical literature of spontaneous cures of cancer. This was the kind of thing that had happened. The patient is diagnosed as having a growth, an abdominal growth, and the surgeon decides to operate. But, the moment he opens up, he finds that the growth is so extensive that there is no question of its removal. Finding that it is so widely disseminated the surgeon decides to sew up immediately. He literally does nothing at all about the growth. However, from that moment sometimes the patient has begun to recover and after a while there has been no further trace or evidence whatsoever of the disease. Such a case may be rare, but it happens. A number of the cases in America belonged to that group—where a surgeon had just performed a laparotomy and no more. Other cases were those in which patients with an advanced malignant growth, some with secondary deposits, developed an intercurrent illness—a fever, or some infectious disease—and from the time they had this other illness, the cancerous condition began to clear up. These medical men who had collected the reports of those cases were quite satisfied that there had been such spontaneous cures or regressions in apparently hopeless cases. We surely must re-examine such evidence and find some explanation of it—for example, among the remarkable mechanisms of immunology. It should deliver us from an overly dogmatic position.

Recent views

There has also been speculation as to the role of immunogens and other physiological and pathological processes. Learned addresses have been delivered on this subject, and to me it is very fascinating, because it is all indicative of the fact that people are now realizing that the whole man is involved and that we must not only consider local manifestations. There are certain other factors. In other words, the tyranny of thinking only in terms of morbid anatomy and pathology is coming to an end.

I have often told a story, which has its amusing element, to illustrate this. I remember when preaching in a certain place I happened to notice during the singing of a hymn that a minister in the town, a man I had known for years, was more or less being carried in by two people, and put into a seat which had been reserved for him. He was obviously crippled with rheumatoid arthritis. They brought him to me at the close of the service and he said he wanted to ask me a question. He had been fortunate at last in getting a bed in the Royal Mineral Hospital at Bath and he wanted to go there for treatment. But to his utter discomfiture he had received an intimation the day before that he would not be admitted to that bed unless he was vaccinated. He was troubled about being vaccinated. He was afraid that in his frail condition this might kill him, and so on. What was my advice? Should he be vaccinated or not? The answer I gave him was that as he was so fortunate in getting a bed in that famous hospital he should go there at all costs. Then I added as a kind of afterthought, "Yes, and in any case you never know what good this vaccination may do you. It may very well clear up your whole condition." We left it at that. I did not see this man for some six months, but, when next I did, I saw him walking towards me perfectly well. I remarked, "Obviously they have very good treatment in the Royal Mineral Hospital at Bath."

He replied, "I never went there."

"Why," I said. "What happened to you?"

His reply was, "Well, as you said, I had such a violent reaction to the vaccination that it seemed to cure me." And it had cured him.

The balance of health and disease

Here is something, surely, that should make us think and think seriously about the whole process of health and disease. Is it not clear that the maintenance of health is a very delicate and sensitive mechanism, that it is a matter of balance? There is a mechanism in the human body that preserves this extraordinary balance between health and disease. I remember fifty years ago reading a great book bearing the title of *Infection and Resistance*, dealing with antibodies and emphasizing the constant fight between disease and the maintenance of health. This goes on not only in the realm of infection but also more generally in diseases such as

31

those to which I have referred. There are forces that are disease producing, and they are held in check by other forces. It is very probable that all this is controlled mainly by the nervous system. Should we not therefore come to the conclusion that disease may be caused by many factors, any one of which may depress this controlling mechanism and knock it out of action temporarily? It may be a shock, it may be an accident, or it may be an infection; it may be one of many other factors. Whichever it is it upsets the mechanism that normally maintains the balance between health and disease and gives the advantage to the disease process.

Are we not entitled also to look at the other side and to say that cures may be the result of very many factors? There are the ordinary means which we use, a variety of drugs, or there may be a direct attack on the infecting organisms. In addition, we have still not altogether abandoned, have we, the building up of resistance? We always knew of that element. In earlier years, we used to send people with tuberculosis to Switzerland and some other centers. What for? Well, to build up the resistance. We had nothing then with which we could attack the bacilli directly, so we concentrated on building up the resistance of the patient. Infection and resistance—that was the balance. And if those treating the condition could push up the resistance, down went the infection and a balance might be restored. As I say, there are examples and illustrations being accumulated in medical literature which are pointing strongly in this direction. And what about the whole question of "the will to live"? I am suggesting that we have tended to be too mechanistic in our outlook upon disease. We have tended to forget the patient and we have tended to forget the delicate balance of the processes which make for health.

The unexpected in medicine

Let me tell one other story which, incidentally, reminds me of one of the greatest blunders of my life in a medical sense! I was preaching in a little chapel in the Vale of Glamorgan for the first time in 1928 on a Tuesday night and Wednesday afternoon and evening. Before leaving for home I was having supper with the old lady with whom I had been put to stay—and she was a real old lady worthy of the name, quite a tyrant in her local community. Suddenly she leaned across the table halfway through the meal and said, "Will you do an old woman a favor?"

I said, "Yes, if I can I will be glad to do so."

"Then," she said, "will you come and preach again next year at these meetings?"

"All right," I said, "I will." We went on eating.

After a while she leaned forward again and she said, "Look here, will you do an old woman another favor?"

I said, "Well, it depends on what it is."

"Oh, it's all right," she said, "you can do it."

I said, "What is it?"

"Will you promise to come and preach at these meetings each year as long as we both live?"

She had already told me she was aged seventy-nine, her skin was more like parchment than skin, and I in my cleverness came to the conclusion that there was no risk at all in acceding to her request, so I entered into the contract.

That was in 1928. Whether you believe it or not, I had to go to preach in that place every year until 1939; and were it not for the second World War and her evacuation to mid-Wales because of the nearby airport, I would have had to go on until 1942 when she died. But this is the point of the story. I think that somewhere about 1936 this poor old lady had a terrible attack of bronchitis and bronchopneumonia. There were no antibiotics in those days, and the sulphonamide drugs were only just coming in. She was desperately ill. Day and night nurses were in charge. All the relatives had been sent for, and they were all convinced, the medical men included, that she was dying. Early one morning, about three o'clock, she suddenly sat up in bed and said, "Give me that calendar, that almanac on the wall!" They all thought, of course, that this was part of her delirium. However she insisted upon having it and they gave it to her. She looked at it and turned over the pages back and fore for some time. This was typical delirium of course! Suddenly she said to the nurse and the relatives, "He will be here in six weeks." She had worked out the date of my annual visit. From that moment she began to get well!

In other words I am trying to show that there are so many factors, which we tend to ignore, which can play upon this delicate mechanism of health and disease. And into this category I would put "faith." I mean faith of any kind. If this view is correct any kind of faith can do it. We must not limit these factors. I have not mentioned the people who seem to have a natural "gift of healing." It is something I do not understand; but it is clear to me that, as many factors can cause disease, so many factors can produce cures. Not only Christian faith, but any kind of faith, faith in "charismatic" personalities, psychological factors, intense emotion, shock, the activity of evil spirits—any one of these factors can do it.

Basic attitudes and principles

So I come to my conclusion. We as Christians must believe in miracles not because of all these things to which I have been referring but because we believe the Bible. Our belief in God puts us into a position in which we have no difficulty in accepting the miraculous and in believing that miracles can happen at any moment in the will and sovereignty of God. What I have been trying to say is of apologetic value, but it should never be the basis of our faith. For us to say, "Ah yes, I can believe in miracles now because of the new scientific outlook, and because of a new way of looking at health and disease," is to me almost a contradiction of the Christian faith. We believe in miracles because we believe the Scriptures, but what I have been saying should be of some apologetic help and value to us and especially in the following way.

We must be very careful that we do not fall into the same

error into which the Roman Catholic Church fell in the case of Copernicus and Galileo. The leaders of that church rejected the facts, you remember, because they did not fit into their theory. We must be very careful that we are not caught at the same point and refuse to recognize facts because our theory regards them as impossible. Indeed I have sometimes had a fear that our dogmatism in these matters is far too similar to that of the Communists and their treatment of Lysenko. We must not ban any findings on purely theoretical or doctrinaire grounds. We must have an open mind and be ready to accept facts and to examine them.

At the same time, I would emphasize that we must still continue to maintain our healthy skeptical and critical attitude to everything that is reported to us. But we must be critical on all sides, not simply on one side. We must have a critical attitude towards the dogmatisms of science, as well as to the often exaggerated claims of certain religious groups. The scientists themselves are doing so today. Everything is so much bigger than men used to think, the possibilities are endless. Man really knows so little. Because we have knowledge in a certain segment we have tended to assume we know all. We do not. "Probability," remember, is the word now, not "determinism."

But, and to me this is the most important finding of all from the theological standpoint, we must not allow our doctrine to be determined by phenomena. This, it seems to me, is the danger today for many good Christians. As I have said earlier, there are many today who seem to be so fascinated by results that they are prepared to abandon what they have always believed. I trust that I have been able to show that there is no need for that.

The rule of Scripture

The Bible itself teaches us to take our doctrine from it alone. Jannes and Jambres, you remember, could reproduce a great deal of what Moses and Aaron did. Our Lord warned that there would be people who would come to him and say, "Lord, Lord, have we not prophesied in thy name, and in thy name have cast out devils? and in thy name done many wonderful works?" He does not dispute the claim nor the facts; but he declares that he will say to them, "I never knew you: depart from me, ye that work iniquity" (Matt. 7:22–23). All along, the Bible instructs us to "prove," to "test" and to "examine" the spirits. The Bible itself teaches us that there are many forces and powers that can produce phenomena and results; and some of them are "evil spirits." Well, how do you decide? All I am saying is that phenomena do not decide. We must not capitulate to phenomena; you arrive at your conclusions on other, on biblical, grounds. Miraculous or supernatural happenings and events do not necessarily validate a ministry, and certainly must never be allowed to determine our point of view. Our Lord's warning still holds, "There shall arise false Christs, and false prophets, and shall shew great signs and wonders; insomuch that, if it were possible, they shall deceive the very elect" (Matt. 24:24).

You may ask me at this point: "Well, how do you decide in any particular case?" It may be extremely difficult. Kathryn Kuhlman is to me one of the most difficult cases of all. She preaches the Lord Jesus Christ and she seems to be correct in her doctrine—that is what makes it difficult. But there are certain other elements in her ministry. I heard her over several days on the radio, while in the U.S.A. in 1969. There are many elements in her ministry about which I would be extremely unhappy. There is an obvious powerful psychological element, even an assumed voice and a very artificial one at that. Then there is a great deal of laughter and joking in her meetings and she boasts of this. Still more basic is the whole question of the teaching of the Bible with regard to the ministry of women!

A commission to heal

So you have to come back to certain general principles which are taught in the New Testament—and, indeed, in the Old. One is that you never find biblical miracles announced several days beforehand. It seems quite clear to me in all the cases which are reported in the Scriptures that what happened was that an immediate commission was given to the man, or to the men, who worked the miracles. For instance, take the case of Peter and John and the man at the Beautiful Gate of the Temple. Likewise Paul with the man at Lystra. The apostles did not know beforehand that they were going to work miracles. I believe they were given an immediate commission. They did not experiment and we are not given any reports of failures in the book of Acts. There is always a kind of certainty, assurance and confidence there. I believe that this was the result of the divine commission that was given to the man concerned. He thus always knew at the time that the particular miracle was going to happen.

One notices, also, that the effect of the working of miracles upon the people was to fill them with a sense of awe and at times of fear. They would say, "We have seen wonderful things today," or ascribe the power to God. In some of the popular healing meetings of today, however, there is laughter and jocularity. The leaders even boast of this. I would say that the Bible teaches that any manifestation of the power of God is awe-inspiring and excludes any spirit of levity or of lightness in one's attitude.

The prayer of faith

I must say just one further word as to the meaning of "faith" in the term of "faith healing." You remember that in the epistle of James it is said that "the prayer of faith shall save the sick" (James 5:15). Then there is the statement in Mark's gospel:

And Jesus answering saith unto them, Have faith in God. For verily I say unto you, That whosoever shall say unto this mountain, Be thou removed, and be thou cast into the sea; and shall not doubt in his heart, but shall believe that those things which he saith shall come to pass; he shall have whatsoever he saith. Therefore I say unto you, What things soever ye desire, when ye pray, believe that ye receive them, and ye shall have them (Mark 11:22–24).

We have all known people who have been trying to work themselves up into this "faith." That, I believe, is the fallacy. I believe the "faith" referred to by our Lord and by James as "the prayer of faith," is again a "given" faith. I put it into the same category as the "commission" that was given to the apostles and others who, in my opinion, have worked miracles since the days of the apostles. Not experimentation, not an announcement on Sunday that there is going to be a healing meeting on Thursday next. They cannot truthfully say that because they do not know. All true divinely wrought miracle is "given"; and "the prayer of faith" is given. No one can work it up; he either has it or he does not have such faith. It partly depends upon a man's general spirituality and his general faith in God and still more upon God's sovereign will.

The biblical attitude

I would conclude by saying this. We must continue to use the usual means in the treatment of sickness and disease. God's customary way of dealing with disease is through these means and methods—through the therapeutic abilities he has given to men and the drugs that he has put in such profusion in nature, and so on. In answer to "the prayer of faith" he may choose to answer apart from ordinary means. But, in addition, we must remember that there is another factor which we have been discussing; we must not be surprised at it, indeed we should be alert with respect to it. We are not to be disturbed in our theology, nor to abandon our biblical positions because of any phenomenon. We are to try and to test them all. We are to explain them, if we can, in the various ways we have considered as we are enabled now to do more easily, perhaps, than in earlier years. But we are still to believe that "with God, all things are possible" (Matt. 19:26).

God can work miracles today as he has done in the past ages. Perhaps we should expect him to do so as the days are darkening and the forces of evil seem to be emerging in an unusually aggressive and potent manner. We must not exclude dogmatically, as we have often tended to do, the manifestation and demonstration of the power of God to heal diseases, or to do anything that he wills and chooses to do. The old exhortation of the apostle Paul to the Thessalonians still stands, "Quench not the spirit. Despise not prophesyings. Prove all things; hold fast that which is good" (1 Thess. 5:19–21). We must not be frightened or become uncritically credulous; but equally we must not "quench the Spirit" or be guilty of reducing the power of God to the measure of our understanding.

CHAPTER 3

On Treating the Whole Man

It has been my privilege and pleasure to be an observer of the profession now for some forty-five years. It has been a most fascinating occupation. Although I left medicine officially in the year 1927, I did not cease to be interested and applied myself to keep up my reading. Some may be surprised at the form which this reading took. I have made it my custom throughout the years to read on Saturday nights the *British Medical Journal*. Let me explain why I made this my practice. I used to prepare sermons on Fridays and Saturdays. When I have thought over material in this way, my mind tends to be overactive with it. So I had to find something which would divert my mind to more leisurely pursuits; and I have revealed the method employed. It worked!

Le me add that I am not commending to you the practice of reading the *BMJ* on a Saturday night, though I think it would do some of you good. For, on the basis of my experience in

Part of an address given at the Quarter-Centenary Dinner of the Christian Medical Fellowship held at the Royal College of Physicians of London on Friday, January 21, 1972.

41

staying with different medical practitioners, I have noticed that not infrequently I see by the side of the desks quite a pile of unopened copies of the *British Medical Journal*! There is another medical publication that for some years I have read, and which I would put into a different category. I did not read *The Practitioner* on a Saturday night. I read it when I was at my best—not as a kind of mild sedative, but as a stimulus. I am very happy to pay tribute to the editor for his monthly notes which I have found to be most stimulating and helpful. They have often given me suggestions for sermons.[1]

Three aspects of recent change

I desire to speak now about the changes which have taken place since the formation of the Christian Medical Fellowship twenty-five years ago. We have been passing through one of the most extraordinary periods in the whole history of the human race. This applies also to the practice of medicine in common with so much else in the national and world spheres. I was reading recently a remark by Peter Drucker, the great American authority on business management. He had explained that the change in the management and running of businesses during the last twenty-five years has been quite astonishing. Up until that time the greatest requisite in the top management in business had been experience. But that is no longer the case. The greatest requirement now is knowledge; this, of course, because of the extraordinary speed of technological development. So now you do not look so much for experience and wisdom in your top men. You must look for knowledge of the latest advances and developments in the application of scientific methods to the conduct of business. Now it seems to me that this fact in many ways has become true in medicine also, and for very much the same reasons.

Then, there is a second change. It is in the kind of problem which is now confronting us. I would subscribe to the view put forward so clearly in a recent book by Sir McFarlane Burnett, *Genes, Dreams and Realities.*[2] I think that he has established the case that the fundamental change which has taken place in the last twenty-five years has been that (with the advent of antibiotics and developments in this department) the diseases which attack men from the outside now are under control. He gives as instance various types of infection. These, he would claim, are more or less under control. The diseases that are not under control, and which are going to constitute the main challenge to medical men in the future, are the internal and degenerative diseases. Most of them are on the increase. They are such diseases as the various forms of malignancy, coronary thrombosis, arteriosclerosis, raised blood pressure and the like. In the future these will constitute the chief problem for medical men.

The third big factor is the advent of state medicine. The National Health Service has been clearly a revolutionary factor—particularly in the realm of general practice. I have had occasion at a previous meeting of this Fellowship to refer to that, and expressed some fears at the changes that are taking place. I have become somewhat more alarmed about these. No longer—speaking generally—can you be sure that a general practitioner will pay a house visit. Everybody has to go to the doctor's office or to the clinic. At times it seems to me to be very bad medicine. I happened to be staying with a doctor on one occasion when a phone call came in that a child was running a high fever. There was at the time, I understood, a mild epidemic of measles in that area. Nevertheless the doctor's message was that they should bring this child up to the clinic. The thought which occurred to me was, "What a good way of spreading the epidemic of measles!" Only today when I was talking about these matters to some friends, one man broke in to the conversation with— "Ah, but, you must add something to that. It is the impossibility of getting any medical attention at the weekend!" Such are some of the changes which have been taking place during these last twenty-five years.

Unwelcome trends

As a result of such considerations I feel there are certain dangers which face the profession at the present time. The first is *professionalism*. It has been an endemic disease, of course, within the profession for many years. The tendency is going to be greater. There are a number of reasons, but one of the chief is the great increase in technological knowledge which leads to an ever increasing specialization. I regard this as a positive danger. As detailed knowledge increases, specialization—and with it professionalism—is going to increase also. A few days ago I was very interested to read a striking article by Marshall McLuhan, that extraordinary Canadian, who stimulates us so much at the present time. He gave us a new definition of a "specialist." I am sure that he was thinking of no one here, and that it does not apply to either physicians or surgeons! But he declared that a specialist is "one who never makes small mistakes, while moving towards the grand fallacy." I commend that definition. It is a salutary reminder.

Technological advance and development is obviously raising a number of problems which must concern any medical man who has any kind of religion, and particularly the Christian religion. I mean that there is a point at which your experimentation should stop. We must remind ourselves of the second part of the great commandment: that you should love your neighbor as yourself. Is there not a danger perhaps of our forgetting that in the interest of science and the acquisition of new knowledge? The poor patient is the one who tends to be forgotten. What right have we to use another human being for the sake of "the advancement of medicine"? Would we ourselves submit always to the procedure which is sometimes applied to a particular patient? Presumably it is never done without the consent of the patient. Is every patient in some situations capable of giving his consent? Does he know enough?

Overlooking the patient

Too many practitioners know more about some detail in the anatomy or pathology of a person than they do about the person himself. While we may talk more of, and pay lip service to, the concept of "the whole man" and "the complete patient," we must be very careful that in fact and in practice we do not forget him.

It is something which we need continually to bear in mind. The patient, the total patient and all that happens to him, is rarely being fully remembered in contemporary practice. Let me quote McFarlane Burnett again. He says,

> An important part of the technological and social crisis of our time is this. The social problems of drug addiction and the more subtle influences of the need of alcohol, tobacco, sedatives, tranquillizers, and the rest, to make intolerable situations acceptable, are tolerated instead of making an effort to change them.[3]

I think that is a very profound remark. Our tendency is to tolerate, just to make these things—these intolerable situations—acceptable without any real thought of radical attempts to change them.

Moral responsibility

Then, thirdly, there is the question of our attitude to immorality and crime. It is important in the following way. You will notice that it is the medical man who is generally called in as the arbiter in these matters. He is regarded as the authority, for example, on the question of "diminished responsibility" and similar matters. At this point the doctor is

45

regarded as the man who can speak with a special authority.

In the past, of course, a kind of general wisdom was deemed, and seemed, to be sufficient. The experienced medical practitioner was a wise old man. Everybody went to him and consulted him. He was a friend of the family and knew everyone. But does his successor *still* know them? It is at such points that our recent developments may be dangerous. It could be argued that one man is as good as another so long as the infective organism has been accurately identified. I suppose that one man is also as good as another in prescribing an antibiotic so long as it is handled with due care. But the point here is that with those diseases which we have mentioned as now increasingly prevalent, it is important to know your patient. You must ascertain the family history, and the more you know about him and his background environment the better you will be able to treat him.

But now another idea is with us. It would seem that you need not even see the patient. Or a doctor may go to a patient whom he has never seen before because he is doing duty this particular weekend. The matter to be dealt with is not so much a patient as the technical point of the particular organism. As for the prescription, I suppose that the computers will soon be doing that for us. The point of our present interest is—where does good medicine come in?

What is it, therefore, that the doctor needs at this point? Clearly he must have a true view of man. At this juncture mere knowledge of medicine is not enough. He must know what man—the whole man—really is. He must know the meaning and nature of life. He must have clear views about death. These are bare essentials. But how are these essentials to be obtained? That is the vital question. And I would not hesitate to assert that it is only a man who is a Christian who conforms to this ideal and who possesses this knowledge.

The bankruptcy of humanism and Freudianism

For general wisdom is no longer enough. It has gone out of fashion, it is not now accepted. It is outmoded. Humanism and moralism are obviously failing completely. It is not difficult to see why. According to the teaching of humanism each man is his own authority, his own standard in the matter of morals. The case against the humanists has been stated perhaps most perfectly by Bertrand Russell, who admitted that he could see no sense nor meaning in life whatsoever. That is inevitably the final position of a humanist. But I feel that humanism and moralism fail supremely at the point where they virtually leave it all to me to solve my own problems. All they seem able to do is to show me the folly of doing certain things, and conversely to commend to me certain other more rational courses of action. But man's real problem is not that he suffers from lack of knowledge. Man is not only an intellect. There are the ultimate problems. To give good advice does not necessarily touch the real problem at all. I would suggest that the contemporary modern world is showing this very plainly.

What, then, of psychology and psychiatry—Freudianism in particular? I would say of Freudianism and, indeed, also of learning therapy and certain other views of psychology— that they share equally in the general hopelessness. I would quote Freud to establish my point here. The following is what he once wrote:

> In all that follows I take up the standpoint that the tendency to aggression is an innate, independent, instinctual disposition in man. The natural instinct of aggression in man—the hostility of each against all and all against the one—opposes the programme of civilization.

But, then, we would ask, where is there any help? There is none at all. It is a state of complete hopelessness, for he declares, "Man, being what he is, instinctively opposes the pro-gramme of civilisation"! In the same context he goes on to say that the instinct of aggression is derived from the death instinct, "the death wish," which he says "we have already found alongside Eros sharing his rule on the earth." Well, surely, that is complete bankruptcy.

I would say that the same applies to many of the non-Christian religions of the world. They are ultimately pessi-mistic and, similarly, offer no real hope. Now this is where the Christian faith seems to me to be absolutely unique. It offers the only hope both for the physician and for the pa-tient. On what grounds can I make such a statement? It is because of its *authority*. Perhaps the greatest need in the world at the moment is that of true authority. It is the key to what is lacking. Every man is doing that which is right in his own eyes. Authority in all forms is being flouted. It is hated. Where are we to find the necessary authority? Time does not permit, but it would be easy to demonstrate that there is no authoritative view of life other than that which you will find in the Bible. The Bible never said that the world would of itself get better and better. No! It was philosophy which said that, and also the pseudoscience of Charles Darwin and T. H. Huxley. The Bible constantly affirms that men will remain what they are until they are willing to come under the Chris-tian influence.

It is widely suggested that there is no such thing as sin, and that everything may be explained away in medical terms. Such a fallacy will endanger the very foundations of the whole of our society and of life throughout the world. We must realistically face the fact that there is positive evil in men. There are some men with whom there is nothing wrong medically, but they are evil and they delight in doing evil. For example, they will do anything for the sake of money and what it can purchase. We must be prepared to assert these things. We must not allow false notions to gain further currency and to ruin the whole of life.

The results

Turning to the future, when you come to consider the question of hope, what hope is there for man? It is here, it seems to me, that is seen the unique message of the Christian faith. It is not merely good advice, it is not mere morality or ethics, nor is it simply a higher view of life. It is a doctrine that gives due place to the real nature and state of mankind. To use biblical terminology, it declares that a man can be "born again," that there can be a radical change in a man's soul. He can become a new man. It is amazing, but it is true. History has its endless examples of it—its striking examples. It is not confined to an elite class—it happens among the common people. Here is hope for the drug addict, the alcoholic, or any kind of individual who has become an utter slave to some particular kind of sin. It has its dynamic—it is "the power of God unto salvation." This is something which is wholly relevant to our calling. As we face the unknown future we can see the kind of problem which is going to arise and to arise increasingly. And I argue that this will become a part of medicine. For we are dealing with a *"whole man."*

I remember some forty-eight years ago, my old chief, Lord Horder, asked me one afternoon whether I would do something for him during his summer vacation. It proved to be this. He had at the time a card index of his patients which was classified solely under their surnames. He was constantly called upon to give a lecture or an address. His problem was that when he wanted to refer to cases he had to rely on his memory. As it happened he had a prodigious memory and he could remember not only the particular cases but often their names, and look the details up on the cards. But he felt that as he was now in his early fifties his memory might fail him. The request was that I would go through his entire system of card indices and make a new supplementary card index beginning with the diseases and passing to the names. In future, when asked to lecture he would refer to the disease references and from the names to the patients' records.

I did this for him. It was one of the best bits of education that I ever received. But what appalled me—and what astounded me—was this. Even in this practice (and he was very often a consultant to a consultant) the diagnosis in well over 50 percent of his cases was "eats too much," "drinks too much," "dances too much," "does not get enough sleep," or "is unhappy at home." He was usually right! I remember raising with him my views about this whole question when I was spending a weekend with him at his home near Petersfield. After I had mentioned it, we argued for the whole of the weekend! My contention was that we should be treating all these people. "Ah," said Horder, "that is where you are wrong! If these people like to pay us our fees for more or less doing nothing, then let them do so. We can then concentrate on the 35 percent or so of real medicine." But my contention was that to treat these other people was "real medicine" also. All of them were really sick. They certainly were not well! They have gone to the doctor—perhaps to more than one—in quest of help.

It was—I know—an elementary anticipation of what today is known as psychosomatic medicine. But I am seriously suggesting that this situation will in the future become increasingly true. Medical men must realize that more and more they will have on their hands the *whole* person to deal with. The various types of new antibiotics and the installation of computers will no doubt be doing a good deal for doctors. But I cannot quite envisage a day when the computer will replace the surgeon. It will clearly never replace the physician! This is an absolute certainty. So the great call to us is that we should become whole men *ourselves* and thereby be in a position to deal with "the whole man" when patients come to us. Let us really understand what is basically wrong. Let us go beyond what technical medicine and the most modern therapy can offer and point men to the Way, the only way in which they can become *whole* men.

CHAPTER 4

Will the Hospital Replace the Church?

The subject on which I have been asked to speak raises a matter of the greatest importance. It confronts not only the members of the medical profession and hospital administrators. It concerns everyone. It will be my duty to substantiate such an unqualified statement. In so far as one's own professional experience is relevant, I am in a position to speak with some confidence. The immediate aspect of the subject before us is that there is today a subtle move to do away with the church. If it succeeds, will it be for humanity's good?

The future of the hospital

That the question should need to be seriously discussed today in medical circles arises from the fact that it has increasingly become a matter for comment in meetings of doctors and hospital administrators. During May of last year (1968) at a conference of the official representatives of the

Part of an address given to the Christian Medical Fellowship at the Royal Commonwealth Society's Hall on Wednesday, March 19, 1969.

associations which are concerned with the hospital services, it was said that:

> The hospital model is now the model to which sociologists are gradually turning their attention . . . As religious causes have waned and society has been secularised, it is the hospital which has succeeded and taken the place of the Church . . . The hospital has had a precarious and clouded history, which is still to be properly written. But, in spite of that history it is now emerging, not as the last refuge for humanity, but as the most important institution of our time.[1]

Speaking some months later at a clinical meeting of the British Medical Association in Cheltenham, Lord Todd commented, "With the general decline in religious observance the doctor has in some measure taken on the role of confidant formerly exercised by the priest . . ."[2] The hospital has already taken over some of the work of the church. Is it destined to do so more and more? The accepted notion seems to be that it will do so. My function, therefore, is to ask whether this is desirable or true.

Historical perspective

The best way to approach the subject will be to look at it historically. But it is just here that the relevant facts are so often forgotten. It is characteristic of the age in which we live. People make false claims because they either overlook or ignore the facts concerning the past.

The fact is that, in western Europe at least, it was the church which founded the hospital. It was Christian people who, out of compassion for the sick and the suffering, felt that something ought to be done. It is very important that we should keep this point before us. It is true that not merely did the church initiate care for the sick, and in one sense by so doing introduced medicine, but she performed exactly the same service in the case of both "Poor Law relief" and education. Let us not forget this. Scientific humanism, which has opposed itself to Christianity, has little that is comparable, and it is important that the humanist should also be reminded of his history. This concern about people—physically, mentally and spiritually—has over the centuries shown itself chiefly among Christians and in the organized church. A number of other groups may, and do, talk a lot about doing good. They generally, however, stop at talking!

It is similarly possible to illustrate this characteristic feature in Christian activity from modern history. In the early days of the developing countries, the building of the hospitals (as, for example, in Africa and parts of Asia), the building of schools, the providing of rules of public health and much else has originally occurred as the result of the concern and the activity of the Christian church. Hence, what was true in more remote history has been repeated, especially in the nineteenth century, in the church's great missionary enterprise.

That is how it began. However, as time passed a certain change took place and these philanthropic functions became separated from their parent. They were, to use the term in the first quotation above, "increasingly secularized." As time passed the practice of medicine, for instance in Europe, was undertaken by individuals who were no longer ordained officers of the church and who sometimes did not even belong to her. They gradually began to take over the care of the sick, or voluntary bodies began to do so, and, as we know, eventually medical care passed into the hands of the state in a national service.

But, at the present time, we are clearly confronted by a new situation. The church's power is waning. The question, therefore, that arises is: can the hospital now take over all the functions of the church? It has already taken over the medical functions. Cannot now the hospital take over all the rest so that the church may finally complete her atrophy and disappear? My object is to prove that this outcome is one that cannot, and should not, happen.

The need for the church

How can I demonstrate this negative? Well, in the first instance, I want to show that this idea, that the hospital could take over the remaining functions, rests on a totally false view of the church. Let me hasten to add, however, that the church herself is in a large measure responsible for this misconception.

What is this false view? It takes many forms. There are some people to whom the church is nothing but a part of our national tradition. Church attendance is a part of "the thing to do," and it is still of some social value in these respects. The usual formalities would not be complete without going to morning service, hoping, of course, it will be suitably brief so that one can adjourn to the sherry party as soon as possible. It is all a part of the social round.

Then a somewhat higher view is that the church is the servant of the state. Her main function is to perform certain things for us. She is useful for a christening, or a marriage or a funeral. The other agencies cannot do that kind of thing quite as well. A civil clerk's office may be all right for legal purposes, but there is something about a church service which, after all, adds dignity to the occasion. So the church remains very useful at such times as a marriage, a christening, and, of course, at death. Further, if there happens to be a war and things are not going very well for the nation, then, of course, the church can organize a national day of prayer.

To move to a higher level, there are a number who believe in the church because, they say, she exercises a good and general moral influence through her teaching. You need discipline in society, they argue, and she really can do very good work in this respect. But, then, some would go even higher still. For, they concede, the church does after all bring in some kind of vague notion of God and a Supreme Being. It is good, they think, that people should have that!

Passing from such general considerations to the more personal, there are many who would suggest that the main function of the church is to provide some kind of therapy. They observe that entering a church has a tranquilizing effect and believe that it has a distinct therapeutic value. From the excitement and distractions of the world you are able to go into a building with "dim religious light" and feel a little bit quieter in spirit. Your nerves become more settled and you have a more comfortable feeling. Then there are the various services, well ordered, well arranged, and with beautiful singing. All that is good for us. It is a pleasant form of escapism. In addition you will probably hear something about love, kindness, good deeds and affection. In this turbulent world all these things are therapeutic and promote mental health. This, we are told, is what the church exists for and she has done it all very well so far.

To look at the matter still more personally, it has been noted that the Christian ministry has a useful place in the common life. The vicar has certainly had great value in the past, because it has been possible for people to rely upon him for sympathy. He is a man who, because he is thought to have not very much to do, will always be ready to listen to you. Most people like to have somebody who is prepared to listen. Those in trouble are greatly helped by just being allowed to talk, and the minister is generally prepared to listen. More than that, he may be able to give some advice or what is now called "counselling." A Roman Catholic can confess his sins to his priest and "confession is good for the soul." The underlying idea is that all this has had a therapeutic value. It has certainly helped people to meet life and its problems

The hospital as a substitute

However, we are now confronted by the new position that people are ceasing to go to church. The question therefore must be put: can the hospital take over all these functions so that the church will no longer be necessary? Again, my answer is that such a view can only be based upon a wrong view of the basic functions of the church. It can only be as a result of an illusion that the hospital can now give these further services—"without the 'mumbo-jumbo', the ceremonial and all the theological dogma." Why do I so firmly reject the suggestion that the hospital can be a substitute? I have sought to classify the answers.

1. Confidences

I would first query the suggestion of the omnicompetence of the hospital, even from the standpoint of fact. This notion is doing a considerable injustice to the doctor of the past, and especially to the general practitioner. It is also granting too much to the Christian minister. Surely, the position has long been that the general practitioner has continually carried out most of the functions that I have been mentioning—apart, of course, from the actual services in a church—more than the minister.

My own personal experience might be brought in at this point. I suppose that the remark which has been made to me more frequently than any other since I have been a minister of religion has been as follows: someone, who has come to consult me, will suddenly add, "Of course, I can tell you this because you are a doctor." The point I am making is that if I had not been a doctor, it seems they would not have dared to tell me. This supports my contention that the general practitioner in the past had been a kind of father figure. He was the adviser of the family—their guide, philosopher and friend. Most of us can remember this type of general practitioner.

2. Impersonalism

Then, in the second place, I come to a point at which I shall have in a measure to express some criticism of "the hospital" and the medical workers who function in it. This aspect of the subject has its elements of irony in relation to the question we are considering, because I have to spend a good deal of my time, and increasingly so I am sorry to say, in listening to people who complain that the doctors are becoming more and more impersonal and mechanical in their treatment of patients. I am not manufacturing such evidence; it is something which the lay public is asserting with greater frankness. They have been given the feeling that they are but guinea pigs. Things are being done to them by their medical advisers, but they themselves have been forgotten as persons.

(a) Poor communication. Another complaint that one often hears—and any minister would confirm this very readily—is that the patient "cannot get anything out of the doctor." If they put questions, or ask for explanations, he becomes impatient. He always seems to be too busy; and the patient and the relatives complain that they cannot get any information out of him. Yet, let me remind you, the proposal is that this same doctor should take over the functions of the clergyman and minister, because someone is needed who is ready to listen and to be very sympathetic! It seems to me that the very crisis through which the medical profession itself is passing today answers the suggestion that the hospital should take over the functions of the church.

(b) Overbusyness. The common impression is that the doctor of today is far too busy. This is particularly true, I am told, of the hospital doctor. Indeed, I hear the same thing about the nurses—that nurses nowadays are not nurses in the old sense. They seem now to be semidoctors, very scientific, very learned, very good at giving injections, good at working out doses and much else, but they seem to have lost

that "motherly" quality which used to characterize a nurse. The nursing is deficient, whereas the scientific knowledge seems to be increasing. One recognizes that this difficulty must arise as medical and surgical treatment becomes more and more scientific and, also, as the staffing problem becomes increasingly acute. My point is that since the hospital is becoming more impersonal it therefore, of necessity, cannot take over the functions of the church.

(c) General practice. But someone may say, "What about the general practitioner?" Well, here again, alas, the position would seem to be very much the same. The development of "group practices" means that the patient finds now that he cannot always have the same doctor. This is particularly true at the weekends. His own doctor is only on duty, perhaps, one in every five or six weekends. If some medical emergency were to occur at that time another doctor will often come in, who probably has not seen the patient before and who does not know anything about the case. Here the personal relationship between doctor and patient is disappearing. In any case the practice of medicine has changed tremendously. In the old days the doctor could and would come in, sit down and have a talk. Nowadays it is a question of form filling, pills, injections or operations; and it is all done so quickly that the patient is out almost before he is in!

If all this is true, then what I am saying is this—that it seems quite clear that, speaking generally, the hospital is in no position to take over even those functions of the church to which I have already referred. Moreover, as general practitioners develop the "clinic" idea more and more—and they are doing so—and are less and less disposed to pay what in the United States are known as "house calls," then the relationship between doctor and patient is going to become still more impersonal. I argue, therefore, that it will become increasingly impossible for the hospital to take over the functions of the church.

3. *The psychiatrists and psychotherapy*

But I come now to something much more basic. The radical, the third, objection which I have to the proposal is what we already know from the work of the psychiatrist Jung. Even he found that it was almost impossible to help patients, especially over the age of thirty-five, who did not possess some kind of religious background. Psychotherapy alone, he found, could not do what was required. There is certainly a school of thought, which is becoming increasingly prominent in the U.S.A., and also more evident in this country, which claims that psychoanalysis has proved to be more or less useless. It is being asserted more and more that the concept of "guilt" must be restored, if the patient is to be helped. Workers such as O. H. Mowrer increasingly find that from time to time they must call in the Christian minister to help them even in the practice of psychotherapy.

This surely is serious, because the psychiatrists were the medical specialists who earlier claimed that they could particularly help in a personal way, in a way that neither the church nor anybody else could do. Even they themselves are now found admitting that in a number of cases their therapy cannot do it. Further, there are others who are entirely opposed to the whole notion of what is called "Freudianism." More of the various types of psychiatric condition are being routinely treated by drugs and mechanical procedures. Even in the sphere of psychiatry the doctor-patient relationship is said to be becoming less evident. We hear less about free association, deep analysis and the long interview.

But quite apart from recent trends, that branch of treatment was really concerned with one type of patient. It was confined to those who are mentally ill in certain defined ways. In other words, it was only concerned about certain aspects of man's life and not with the man himself and his basic problem.

The function of the church

Here I come to a fourth argument, which, to me, is the really vital one. What, in fact, is the true function of the Christian church? It must be considered from two points of view—the primary, essential function of the church on the one hand, and what may be called the subsidiary "by-products" or "incidental functions" on the other. It is an essential distinction if we wish to keep this subject in due perspective.

Those who are familiar with the New Testament will know that this distinction is something which was very evident in the ministry of the Lord Jesus Christ himself. There are two aspects of his ministry: he came in order primarily "to seek and to save that which was lost." Then there was also his healing ministry and his helping people in other ways.

Christ's primary purpose and function was neither to heal the sick nor to bring relief in other ways. He certainly did all that, but it was not what he had primarily come to do. The gospel of John emphasizes this very clearly by referring to his miracles always as "signs." He did these other things because he had a heart of love and of compassion; but he had not come into the world for this purpose. Also, the miracles or "signs" were meant to confirm the fact that he was who he claimed to be. The healing part of his ministry was something that was almost incidental. His primary object was to accomplish something for all mankind which he alone could do. This is crucial.

What, I say, was true of him in his ministry is equally true of the Christian church. The authentic task of the church is not primarily to make people happy; it is not to make people healthy; and it is not even to make people good. The church, of course, is concerned about making people good, and that they should be happy; yes, but that is not her primary function. This fact is perfectly plain, not only in the Bible itself, but in the great periods of the Christian church when she

62

really has been functioning fully as the church. Her essential task is to restore men to the right relationship with God.

Hence the real business of the church is not something which is man-centered. It is God-centered. This is a vital distinction. The hospital and the state can take over many, if not most, of the indirect activities of the church. But they cannot, and never will, take over the primary function. It is because people have fallen into the habit of substituting the "secondary functions" for the main function of the church that we have come into all the confusion. There are even many who claim triumphantly that the political parties have also taken over the functions of the church. It has particularly been so in Wales. During the last century the Welsh chapels were the center of the people's life in almost every respect—culturally, as well as every other. Then a great change took place. The politicians took over, especially the socialists, and they drew away the people from the chapels. This was to a great extent due to the fact that so many of the preachers had become politicians rather than preachers. If you think of the Christian church—and as a result of the impressions received from the television and radio no doubt many do—as primarily an organization to preach pacifism and socialism, to protest against war and apartheid and other such things, then you are perfectly entitled to say that all this can be done without the church and without all that is associated with its life.

The real issue

The basic element in my case is that the church's primary function is to restore men to a right relationship with God, and this is something, I assert, which only it can ever perform. In the true teaching of the church, it is man himself who is the central problem. The moment a person realizes this, he also realizes at once that this is something which is true of each individual. I would therefore confront the physician, the surgeon, the psychiatrist, the administrator, or whoever he may be, who proposes that he can take over the church's function, with some such reminder as the following: "You cannot do so, because you yourself need what the church alone can supply. You yourself are as much in need as those whom you think you can help. Everybody is in need at this point—it is universal."

Let me put it in another way. Man's real problem is not simply that he is sick, but that he is a rebel. Now here again is a crucial distinction. The current notion is that humanity is sick. And of course it is sick, very sick indeed. The real question, however, is why is it sick? The basic answer of the Bible and the church, when she is really preaching the Bible, is that man's ultimate problem is not the sickness. That is only a symptom, or a complex of symptoms. It is a manifestation of something much deeper and more serious.

The consequences

The central message of the church is that man is a rebel against God. All our troubles result from that fact—all of them, without any distinction. It is especially true of those symptoms which are most obvious in the life of the world today. Man has made himself autonomous. He does not recognize anything above and beyond himself. He regards himself as the greatest factor in the universe. You must have read recently of the claim that man is now in a position even to be a "creator." Because man has become autonomous he has inevitably become self-centered, and self-centeredness always leads to certain consequences. If I am a "god," nobody must be allowed to reduce my status. But the other man also regards himself as a "god," so that we are both very sensitive about our "powers" and hence we are constantly overprotecting ourselves. This paves the way for jealousy and envy. It also leads to aggressiveness and aggression. All this in turn, of course, leads to overwork. A man aims at a position, then when he has achieved it, he is afraid of losing it, for "uneasy lies the head that wears a crown." And so we overwork and we become overtired. We become deeply involved in what is known as the rat race. We begin to feel the strain and here is the central problem of modern society.

In addition to all that, and on another level, there is the undercurrent of lust, desire and passion. It does not matter how scientific a man may be in his work, he is still a man. He has certain primitive instincts within him which are much more powerful than his mind and his will. The fact that any-one is intellectually an able man does not mean that he can control himself and his own passions. All this leads in the long run to overtiredness, restlessness, a sense of guilt, re-morse and finally a sense of failure. Hence there is the resort to pep pills, tranquillizers, hypnotics or an excess of alcohol. It does not matter which of them it is; experience empha-sizes that so often it all ends up in a sense of futility and the despairing question, "Is it worth it all?"

Palliation or treatment?

This is the position, and surely medicine can do nothing about all this except to palliate the symptoms. I am not, of course, suggesting that this is a bad thing to do in itself. It is quite right to do what we can to palliate symptoms, yet with this qualification—that a true diagnosis has already been made. Sometimes it is a very dangerous act to palliate symp-toms. If you are confronted by a man in acute pain, say ab-dominal pain, and you give him a pain-relieving injection without first doing all that is possible to discover the cause, then I suggest that it is bad medicine! Every well trained medical student and qualified doctor should be in no doubt about it. But, I suggest, that in moral and spiritual matters we are continuing to do just that and on a national scale!

All the palliatives, and all that the hospital can do, and all the medical profession at its best can do in these matters of which we are speaking, is really only to deal with symptoms. They are not able to face up to the real issue. Centuries ago the central diagnosis was surely put, once and for all, by St. Augustine. Having tried many palliatives, he at last came to this crucial conclusion before God: "Thou hast made us for Thyself, and our hearts are restless until they find their rest in Thee." That is the need, surely, of modern man and his society today. The primary function of the church is radically to deal with that. It is the church alone which can do so.

The nature of man

We must continue to ask—what basically is man? It is the teaching of the Bible alone that goes straight to the basic issue. Is he only an animal? Well, if so, what right have you to complain that he is behaving like an animal. He is clearly demonstrating this for you. You should not be surprised, and there is nothing for you to do about it.

But, surely, he is not merely an animal. Here we must emphasize the prevailing fallacy. It is overlooked that, in fact, he is a creature who has been made in the "image and likeness of God." There is something about him which transcends everything else in the universe. He is God's representative in the world. He is what the Bible terms "a living soul." He has within him a longing for "an ampler ether, a diviner air." He has a sense of incompleteness. He has a sense of something bigger and greater than himself. He cannot define it. But deep within him there it is! The church alone can enlighten him about its nature. It is God! He was made for God and appointed "lord of creation." He does not, however, find his companionship and communion in nature. No, because he is too big for that and the world at its best cannot satisfy him. It can give him much, but still there remains the void about which we have earlier spoken.

It is the church alone, I say, that can give the real answer. And the answer is that mankind needs God. Men in general do not recognize this. It is the business of the church to tell them. A given individual may feel perfectly happy. He may be born with an equable nature—some people are. Just as you can have nice dogs or cats so you can have nice men and women! But there they are, happy up to a point. But the evil day will come. They need to realize the truth about themselves as men, they need to know God. They need something altogether beyond themselves. God has put certain laws into man's nature, and all his unhappiness finally results from his resisting the law of his nature, that is, from fighting God. We stubbornly object to the claims of the Highest and set ourselves up as petty authorities.

The Golden Rule

The first part of God's law for men is: "Thou shalt love the Lord thy God with all thy heart, and with all thy soul, and all thy mind." The second part is, "Thou shalt love thy neighbour as thyself" (Matt. 22:37, 39). There are many who object today, "Surely I can love my neighbor as myself without loving God?" But this is where they go wrong, they cannot. In stating these two aspects of God's commands, Christ put them in that order because logically it is the inevitable order. To be able to "love thy neighbour as thyself" implies that you have first to achieve a right view of yourself. If you have not that, then love of your neighbor—and experience bears this out—will, of necessity, be a very poor thing. Left to ourselves we cannot love in this way. And the natural reaction of most men is, "Why should I do it?" No, the only hope for the community, as well as for the individual, is that we all equally submit ourselves to God and come to the realization that we are meant to function under him.

The moment a man realizes that he is only a pilgrim in this world, that finally he has to die and to face God, and that there is all eternity before him, his whole outlook on life changes. Immediately the church is able to tell him that, although for so long he has been so wrong, he can be forgiven. The church's central message is the doctrine of forgiveness, based upon the fact that "God so loved the world, that he gave his only begotten Son, that whosoever believeth in him should not perish, but have everlasting life" (John 3:16). It is the crucial message of the fact of the Son of God's coming into the world in order to bear our sins and their punishment, to reconcile us to God, and to give us a new birth, a new life and a new outlook. This is not mere theory. The long history of the church is filled with proof of it. We can thank God that some of us know something about it in practice. To say that, to teach that, and to bring people to a realization of it—that is the primary function of the Christian church. She alone can undertake it.

Conclusion

So, to sum up, the hospital, quite rightly in my opinion, has taken over the healing of the sick, the healing of the body, and, in a measure, the healing of the mind. The state has also taken over the administration of social relief, education and much else. There is no objection to all this, so long as it is well done. But the moment that hospital or state say that they can take over everything, including the spiritual, and that the church has become unnecessary, they reveal evidence of their ignorance on the grand scale. They not only fail to discern the true nature of the church, but reveal a disastrous gap in their understanding of the nature of man himself—themselves included. They fatally neglect the only power that can enable man to function truly, that is the gospel of Jesus Christ, "for it is the power of God unto salvation to every one that believes" (Rom. 1:16).

CHAPTER 5

The Doctor as Counsellor

There is a very definite impression in the minds of the lay public that a doctor can be trusted with confidences more than anybody else. It seems to me that they believe that they can trust him, rather than the Christian minister, because he has always been the repository of his patients' detailed personal matters. And this I think is going to be increasingly the case. Many of the churches are losing their congregations. It is no longer the custom for people to go to church as they once did. So it is no longer the practice for people to go, with the same frequency as they used to do, to see a Christian minister.

The family doctor

Now I am old enough to remember the days when the doctor was a counsellor in a wider sense; and this was especially true of the old type of family doctor. He was almost invari-

From *Guidelines* No. 24. Part of an address to clinical medical students at BMA House on Thursday, February 3, 1972.

ably a friend of the whole family. When he went into the homes he realized that he had brought many of these people into the world, and they had grown up with him. He knew them intimately and they all knew him as "guide, counsellor and friend." People would turn to him for advice; and he was highly successful in this respect. It might be that many such doctors were not Christians at all, but they had developed a kind of general wisdom. They were men who met life in the raw, they were men of experience, and from time to time they were present at crises in the lives of these families.

I may be wrong, but I have a distinct impression that this is no longer the case. I hear, very frequently, complaints at the present time about the National Health Service and about the difficulty of getting a doctor to visit a home. This is something that will have to be argued out in the future. I believe it to be a tragic loss—this intimate contact between doctor and the patient and his whole family life. It is a need that will become more prominent, because people will be crying out for it.

Whether there will have to be some new kind of specialization in this respect I am not sure. I would argue that the general practitioner, the man who practices medicine in general rather than a specialty, is still the man who is in a unique position to counsel people. It will be something that will be needed more and more because we are facing problems of a more acute form at the present time, through the extraordinary technological developments and new factors which have arisen within our own lifetime. For example, I believe that it is correct to say that at the present time somewhere around 45 percent of the hospital beds are occupied by psychiatric patients of various types. The sheer pressures of life and the pace at which we are all living tends to accentuate the human dilemma.

The doctor's personality

I believe that the best way of approaching our theme is to take a particular case, to discuss it together and to work it out. There are certain absolute essentials. The first is the doctor himself. We must start here. Counselling is not something outside the personality of the doctor, it is a part of it. There is a sense in which any kind of man can prescribe, let us say, penicillin. It does not matter whether he has a good or bad character. In the case of a straightforward condition such as an infection, it is a question of early diagnosis and—if possible—identifying the infecting organism, and then prescribing. But when we come to counselling, the doctor himself is a vital part of the situation. He is not doing something outside himself. He is giving something of himself and his experience, and there is an exchange taking place between the patient and himself. Hence the most important thing of all in counselling is the character and personality of the counsellor.

The quiet mind

What is the greatest essential in a counsellor? I would say that it is a quiet mind and that he is at rest in himself. You will remember how our Lord put this on one occasion—"Can the blind lead the blind? shall they not both fall into the ditch?" (Luke 6:39). In other words, if a man is in trouble with himself, and is restless, he is really in need of counselling himself. How can he give useful counsel to another? The first requisite, therefore, in a counsellor is that he himself is possessed of a quiet mind, a mind that is restful. It is at that point, of course, that the importance of the Christian faith comes in. I am prepared to defend the proposition that no man ultimately can have a quiet mind, a heart at rest, and "at leisure from itself" unless he is a Christian. He needs to know a true peace within—the peace of God which is able to

71

keep "both mind and heart." For the patient comes in an agitated troubled condition and can detect if there are similar manifestations in the counsellor.

Christian doctrine

The second need is an understanding of Christian doctrine. What do I mean? A man can be a Christian and still be very defective in his understanding of Christian doctrine and the basis of Christian peace. When anyone takes up the role of counselling he is in the sphere of daily living and practice. People will come to him with problems. How is he going to counsel them? He himself may have had a wonderful experience of conversion, but that in itself does not necessarily enable him to be a good counsellor. I have sometimes known it to be a hindrance. For example, when Christians have come suffering from various forms of spiritual depression they have been treated by other Christians to a thumping slap on the back and the suggestion—"Pull yourself together, cheer up!" But that may do more harm than good, because it is the one thing which the poor patient cannot do at the time. I have known problems exaggerated and aggravated by this sheer lack of knowledge of skilled "doctoring." It is not enough to have had the experience yourself. You need to reason with people and to take them on step by step, until you have brought them out of their difficulty. But you can only do that if your answers, and your whole approach, are governed by an understanding of the Christian life as a whole. It is a whole life.

The approach to a patient

Coming now to the actual handling of the patient, the first basic requisite is patience. This is, of course, a manifestation of the quiet mind. If you are not able to exercise such patience you will be a very bad counsellor. If you appear to be

72

only half-listening, and give the impression that your mind is somewhere else, and that you think that the interview is a waste of time, you will do no good at all. You must be ready to give yourself to listening. Above everything else you must listen to what the patient says. It is astonishing to note the way in which people are helped merely by having someone who will listen to hem.

Let me illustrate. One day Sir Thomas, later Lord Horder, physician to St. Bartholomew's Hospital, was asked to see a very distinguished patient—a Duchess. The local practitioner had written a letter of introduction and had told him that he was sure that there was nothing really wrong with her, though she thought there was. She had been to see most of the distinguished consultants in Harley Street, as well as on the Continent. But she felt no better, and somebody had suggested Horder. As it happened, the previous consultation before the arrival of the Duchess had been a most interesting medical problem in differential diagnosis at which Horder excelled. This particular patient had been misdiagnosed and Horder had discovered what was really the matter with him and could see that he could be cured.

On the arrival of the Duchess, Horder simply said, "Please tell me about your symptoms and experience. I will ask you a question now and again. But just take your time and tell me." So she began. While she was talking he was busy writing a letter to the doctor of the previous patient. Now and again he would stop and put a question to her. Then he would go on writing to the doctor concerned with the previous case, and the Duchess went on speaking. This continued until he had finished writing the letter to the previous doctor, giving him the diagnosis, his reasons for it and the suggested treatment. Then he told the Duchess to go on a bit longer and added, "Well, now, this is most interesting." He then proceeded to examine her chest and to take other steps to exclude the presence of what might be lurking signs of any serious condition.

At the end of the consultation she said, "You know, Sir Thomas, I am sure that you are going to cure me."

"Oh," he said, "how do you know that?"

She replied, "You are the first doctor who has taken the trouble to listen to me!" (In one sense this is not a good illustration of what I want to say; for Horder was not really listening, but in that particular case there was nothing to listen to!) He had won her confidence in a way which no one else had and he was able to deal successfully with her hypochondria.

He had acted on the assumption that there was nothing seriously wrong with her, yet there was obviously something wrong, otherwise she would not be bothering all these doctors. He was able to help because she received the impression that he was patiently following her explanations. I cannot emphasize this point too strongly. It takes us well on the road to solving one of the common conditions which is so widespread today.

Genuine sympathy

The attitude required also includes an element of sympathy. You must not be impatient with people, even when you are reasonably sure that they are neurotic, for the symptoms are very real to them. To you it may be nonsense, but you should be careful because you may one day have subjective symptoms yourself! When I was still practicing medicine, for some reason a considerable number of ministers and clergy would come to consult me. I arrived at the conclusion that they were mostly neurotic because of their complaining of the same symptoms—vague indigestion, headaches and inability to sleep, and so on. I began to think that these preachers were "a pack of neurotics." But I had not been more than nine months in the ministry when I began to notice the similar symptoms in myself. I had become a "neurotic"! In other words there are tensions in the ministry—the very nature of the work tends to produce them. So learn not to be impatient with the person consulting you. It is all very real to him in his daily experience and in his efforts to overcome the debilitating effects of the type of life which he has to lead. I seriously question whether anyone has a right to be practicing clinical medicine who has no real concern for persons and for people.

Humility

My next point is a negative one. Unfortunately it is necessary to add it. Do not cultivate an air of great knowledge! I have known a good deal of damage to come from this failing in a young practitioner. A patient comes to him under the impression that he or she has some serious condition. He soon satisfies himself that this fear is unwarranted. But the well-informed new sage—ostensibly with the best motives—begins to discuss points of differential diagnosis with the patient, and to give a great display of knowledge in the process. The steps are anxiously followed by the patient. The genius goes on, "Oh, no, it isn't A, though it might have been B, or even C. But it isn't that!" Do you know to what this kind of behavior leads? The poor patient begins to imagine that he or she may be suffering from every single one of these possibilities! The doctor has simply introduced new problems to the patient. I heard the other day of a small child who had fallen from a baby carriage, and a little later a small hematoma had appeared. The anxious mother informally consulted a doctor, who as it happened was a pathologist. He should not have answered her questions, but he did. While assuring the mother that he thought that there was nothing seriously wrong, he went on to say that it might be this or that or develop into this or that. When the swelling changed color and the child proved a bit fractious, the mother was beside herself with anxiety concerning the "fracture," "internal hemorrhage," "thrombosis" and all the possibilities.

The patient's conscience

Another point will become more relevant in present conditions. The counsellor needs to be very careful that his primary concern is not his own conscience. This may at first sound strange and contradictory of Christian standards. It is, of course, a particular difficulty for Christian doctors and counsellors. Increasingly, the patients will come with moral problems and their accompaniments—contraception, abortion and the like. Here lurks a danger. I am prepared to argue that if your main concern is the preservation of your own conscience you are likely to be a very bad counsellor! The reason is that the man who is afraid of giving the wrong advice, or advice which he may feel is not Christian for himself (with an eye on his own conscience) tends to be legalistic. He also becomes cold and mechanical. Anyone who is legalistic in attitude forfeits his value as a trusted counsellor. What is needed is great patience and sympathy, and the power to put oneself in the patient's situation. The adviser must not hold to his own rigid position, otherwise the patient will simply become a tangent to a closed circle. The adviser may end by feeling that he has taken the "Christian stand" and said all that was right. He may feel happy; but he may by this very fact have left the patient in extreme misery. This is obviously bad counselling.

The point is that we must be very careful not to foist our opinions on others. The counsellor is not a dictator, he is simply there to give help. While he may give his views and, with care, put them quite strongly if asked, yet all that is put to the patient must be in the spirit of real sympathy, love and understanding. As counsellors we must never be in the position of dictating to another person's conscience. We have no right to imagine ourselves as "the conscience" of another! We are there to share with those who consult us experience, knowledge, wisdom and suggestions concerning the way of cure. There are, unfortunately, Christians who feel it their duty to impose their own legalistic views on others. Our business, however, is to persuade, never to force. We must always be careful to avoid condemnation—especially in the case of a sick or agitated person. If the plain truth of the situation comes home to the patient that is one thing; but it is not our place to condemn.

The diagnosis

The above points are mostly concerned with background attitudes, but they are all very important. Without them, indeed, what follows would be out of perspective. Having ensured that the approach has been right, we come to the actual diagnosis. If you cannot make a diagnosis you cannot finally help your patient. Here again lies the importance of an accurate knowledge of the facts, the facts of life and the spiritual facts. They all come together here. To me the thing that is needed above everything else at the present time is an accurate textbook which deals with the borderland where the spiritual, the psychological and the psychiatric meet. This is the most difficult sphere of all in the practice of medicine and in Christian pastoral work. I have thought about it for some forty-five years, for ministers have been in the habit of sending people to me and explaining, "I don't know what to think of this case, is it a spiritual or a psychological one?" There is really no adequate textbook on this problem; and it is very important from every standpoint. Much time will be lost if you cannot differentiate. You will be unhelpful to the person who is confronting you and perhaps even harmful.[1]

The following may illustrate what I mean. When I arrived at Westminster Chapel one Sunday afternoon about five o'clock, two senior church members came into my vestry. I could see by their faces that they were troubled. I asked,

"Well, what is the matter with you two?" They explained that they had been talking to a man for some three hours about his spiritual difficulties; and they had virtually exhausted themselves, but to no effect. On enquiring the name, I found that the man to whom they had been talking in spiritual terms was a poor fellow who had had electric shock treatment three times! He was a case of manic-depression in one of his typical phases. They had fallen into the well known trap. Because he had come to the Chapel and had asked spiritual questions, they had assumed that he was a spiritual case.

One of the first things one learns in practice in relation to these borderline areas, is to make a broad general diagnosis of the category into which the patient falls. Then one can begin to apply the particular line of treatment. This is not as easy as it may sound. The patient's reactions to what you are seeking to do is sometimes surprising, because his mind has not been trained into the approach of the doctor.

Informing the patient

Normally the patient should not be told too much in detail. "A little learning is a dangerous thing." It is good for doctor and patient when the new practitioner beginning his life's work has passed through this stage. I remember very well how, when I began working as a medical student in the wards and was beginning to learn clinical medicine, I developed acute pleurisy after reading a textbook. Of course I had not got it. But I had all the symptoms and they were all very real to me! Now if this was so with a medical student (who presumably was intelligent!) how much worse may this be with the public in general? The point is that you must either say very little, or you must say everything! Since the patient cannot be given everything—and time alone forbids this—I maintain that the less you say in detail the better. The older type of practitioners were men of few words, but they mostly satisfied their patients at these points. You may say that there was a good deal of "mystique" about the old doctor. But all patients are human and a little mystique now and again is necessary.

CHAPTER 6

The Christian and the State—With Special Reference to Medicine

We are first and foremost Christians and only secondarily medical men. For is it not true that we are incidentally medical, whereas socially we are Christian? Hence, the way to approach this problem—as any others which are complicated—is to work from the general to the particular. Most of our difficulties arise because we make a direct attack on problems. We then get into confusion because the local circumstances assume too great a proportion and we lose sight of our first principles. So here we must start with the Christian in his general relationship to the state, and then, having understood that, we can consider his particular relationships in medicine.

The wider setting of the problem

A further classification is necessary. The Christian's relationship to the state is only one aspect of a still larger ques-

From a verbatim report of an address to members of the Christian Medical Fellowship on October 24, 1957, in the Hall of the Medical Society in London.

tion, that is, his relationship to life in general in this world. Now, I consider that evangelical Christians are particularly prone to go astray on this whole matter; they are more prone to do so than other Christians. The reason is not far to seek. It is because we place great emphasis upon personal salvation. This is what marks us out as "evangelical." We realize that the essential thing is that a man should have a personal experience of the Lord Jesus Christ; indeed, we are doubtful whether he is a Christian at all, if he has not that. Hence our first emphasis is always upon the personal experience of salvation, and, because of it, the danger always is to think that such an experience comprises the whole of Christianity—that it starts with personal salvation and that it ends with personal salvation.

There are a number of texts that tend to encourage us in this wrong tendency. We misunderstand them, of course, but taken out of their context they do tend to lead us to make wrong conclusions. Here is one of them: "My kingdom is not of this world" (John 18:36). Our Lord constantly spoke about his kingdom. He had come to establish it. People enter into his kingdom and he says of it that it is not of this world. At this point the evangelical Christian is liable to deduce that Christianity has nothing at all to do with this world. The text by itself encourages what is already an inherent tendency in him, to regard Christianity as purely spiritual and experimental, and to think that Christianity has no wider applications at all. Another well known text is used: "Come out from among them, and be ye separate" (2 Cor. 6:17). This becomes pressed to the point that the Christian has virtually nothing to do with the state at all. Some people, as you know, would say that it is very wrong for a Christian to take any part in politics. Some would say it is wrong for him even to exercise the privilege of voting at an election. There have been Christians who have carried these particular doctrines to an extreme of saying that we are to be really separate and

82

have nothing at all to do with this world. Similarly, Revelation 13 has often been misunderstood in the same way. The two "beasts" which are depicted there are interpreted as representing the state as something entirely evil, which is utterly opposed to the Christian. Therefore, obviously he should have nothing at all to do with the state.

It is no new problem. Christians were troubled by such doubts from the beginning. That is why, in the New Testament epistles, there is a good deal of attention paid to the relationship between masters and servants. Some of the early Christian converts, who were slaves, began to argue: "Because I am a Christian, because I have been born again and because the apostle Paul says 'if any man be in Christ, he is a new creature,' and 'old things are passed away and behold all things have become new,' I am no longer in the same relationship as I previously was to my master and employer." The apostles Peter and Paul both had to deal with the matter. Their converts had jumped to the wrong conclusions. Many argued in the same way with regard to husband and wife. Why was 1 Corinthians 7 ever written? Was it not because of this very point, that a husband was tending to argue that because he had been converted, and his wife had not, he should no longer live with her? The old order had finished and had gone. He was in a new world and a new creation. So the apostle was compelled to discuss the matter. We in our time are only meeting the same difficulties as were felt in the first century and as have often since been felt in the long history of the church.

We need to be aware of the lack of thought on this matter in recent years, and the failure to grasp first principles. This applies not only to the state in general, but to individual relationships also. Some who say it is wrong to serve the state because it is not Christian are yet prepared to go into partnership with a non-Christian; it does not seem to occur to them that they are inconsistent from their own standpoint. They also fail to see that their fellow directors in a business and in many big concerns are no more Christian than the state!

Major Scripture references to the state

There is one key statement in the Old Testament, which is important because it is quoted again in the New Testament: "When the Most High divided to the nations their inheritance, when he separated the sons of Adam, he set the bounds of the people according to the number of the children of Israel" (Deut. 32:8). A much more important statement, of course, is that which was made by our Lord himself when replying to the trap set by the Herodians. The gospels record that,

> The Pharisees took counsel how they might entangle him in his talk. And they sent out unto him their disciples with the Herodians, saying, Master, we know that thou art true, and teachest the way of God in truth, neither carest thou for any man: for thou regardest not the person of men. Tell us therefore, What thinkest thou? Is it lawful to give tribute unto Caesar, or not?

Our Lord asked them to show him a penny. He looked at it and said,

> Whose is this image and superscription? They say unto him, Caesar's. Then saith he unto them, Render therefore unto Caesar the things which are Caesar's; and unto God the things that are God's (from Matt. 22:15–21).

That is a crucial passage. There are others, for example, the apostle Paul's statement in Acts 17:26 in his sermon at Athens (which is really a quotation of the Deuteronomy reference above). But the classical statement will be found in the epistle to the Romans: "Let every soul be subject unto the higher powers. For there is no power but of God: the powers that be are ordained of God" (Rom. 13:1). And, then, in 1 Peter 2:13–18 the apostle Peter deals with the relationship of masters and servants and the duty of all men to honor the emperor.

In addition to the above passages in which teaching is explicit, there are certain others in which it is implicit. There is teaching implied in the actions of certain of God's people. Here are some of the important ones: first there is Daniel 3, where three young men were cast into the burning fiery furnace because they would not bow down to the image. Then in chapter 6 we are told of the trap which was laid for Daniel himself, by a proclamation which was ordained that people were only to pray to one specified god, and not to the other gods. Daniel ignored it; he went on praying three times a day with his window open to Jerusalem as he had done heretofore, with the result that he was cast into the den of lions. Similarly, we have Acts 4 recording that the disciples were prohibited to preach in the name of Christ, and cast into prison for disobeying the order. Then there is in Acts 16 the apostle Paul's refusing to go out of prison until the magistrates, who had imprisoned him wrongfully, had come themselves to let him out. Finally, we read in Acts 25:11 of the apostle Paul appealing to Caesar, demanding his right as a Roman citizen to appear before the emperor himself that he might state his case and be protected against unfair treatment. These are some of the more important Scripture statements.

The Christian doctrine of the state

What is the essential teaching? It is that God is the Creator, as well as the Savior. Many evangelists appear to overlook this. There is a grave danger among them of what might be called a "Jesusolatry," a tendency to speak exclusively in terms of the Lord Jesus Christ. Everything is concentrated on his person, prayer is offered only to him and not to God the

85

Father. From one point of view and in one setting, of course, that is perfectly right. We know that our salvation is in him. But what often is forgotten is that all he did was precisely because he was sent by God to do it. He died in order that his death might bring us to God, not to himself. There are numerous passages which state that fact unambiguously, for instance, "God was in Christ, reconciling the world unto himself" (2 Cor. 5:19).

These considerations concerning the state must start with God, and we must remember that God is the Creator as well as the Savior. The particular reason for emphasizing this is because God has not abdicated his interest in the world. It is wrong to think that God is interested only in Christian people. Our Lord himself taught this clearly when he reminded us that God "maketh his sun to rise on the evil and on the good, and sendeth rain on the just and on the unjust" (Matt. 5:45). This is still God's world, though it is in sin, and though man has fallen, God is certainly doing something special for his own people whom he is calling out of this world (in the spiritual sense) into his kingdom. But this fact must never be interpreted as meaning that he has turned his back upon the world as such. He is still interested, and it is because of his interest that he has ordained certain measures with respect to the world in general.[1]

For example, God has ordained the family as the fundamental unit of society. That is his ordinance and not man's. It remains absolute whether a man is a Christian or not. Christianity does not interfere with the divine regulations for marriage, the family and the state. The state is not the outcome of man's ideas. Aristotle taught that man evolved the state, and others—for example, French political writers—in other ways taught it also. But it is a fallacy which many Christians tacitly believe. We who accept the biblical teaching and the biblical authority must take note of its teaching when it tells us that it was God who has divided up the bounds of the nations. It is he who has determined states, however much intrigue and strife may seem to prevail. He ordained "the powers that be."

He is said to have ordained states, kings and princes. It is very difficult to tell from Scripture, however, which particular form of state is regarded as the ideal. That does not seem to matter. Government of some pattern is ordained by God and it derives its authority from God. The state has been given an authority by God for particular purposes.

The functions of the state

What then is the purpose of the state? What are its functions? The first is to restrain evil. It is because sin has come into the world that the state has become necessary. A chaotic element has come in. Life, however, still needs to be ordered. Evil is a vicious thing which tends to destroy and to disrupt and one of the main functions of the state is to put a bound upon evil. The apostle Paul declares this in Romans 13. He says that the state is for the punishment of evildoers and for the praise of them that do well—that is why the magistrate bears the sword. I know that we as evangelicals may say, "Well, it does not matter very much if a man is not saved whether he is good, bad or indifferent." From the point of view of the full teaching of the Bible that is wrong. This man must be caused to live within bounds and that is one of the reasons why God has ordained the state. It is part of our business as Christians to teach that.

The second function of the state is to preserve order. It is, in other words, to remind people that God is over all. But what is the sphere of this authority of the state? What is the sphere in which the state operates? This is of special importance today in a number of respects. The answer, as I understand the biblical teaching, is that the sphere of the state is confined to our external actions. There is nothing in the Bible to indicate that the state has a right to control my opinions, whether they are religious or whether they are political, whether they are philosophical, whether they are scientific or whether they are medical. In fulfilling its functions to preserve order, to restrain evil and to make life harmonious, the state has no right to interfere in the realm of man's mind and his thinking. If the state attempts to usurp the right to control our thinking, then our relationship with it becomes critical.

The Christian attitude to the state

Our duty is to recognize and respect the state as of divine ordination. The great Protestant reformers, particularly John Calvin, who was the most systematic thinker among them, and John Knox, emphasized this fact; Luther also did—up to a point. Church and state, they said, have a divine origin and must not be regarded as a contrivance with which the Christian has nothing to do. "You are wrong," they said, "if you think that because God has set the church to save men's souls, to feed them spiritually and to provide fellowship for them, that it can virtually dispense with the state. The church is the kingdom of God in its present form. But, do not forget that God has equally ordained the state for his own ends and another purpose, namely, to restrain sin in the world until it is finally judged and put away." The two spheres operate side by side and not in alliance.

The reformers did not believe in the union of church and state, but in two spheres of God's action and the "two realms." There has been a great deal of argument and discussion concerning the proper relationship between the two. The church of Rome declares that the church is over the state. The Erastians said that the church is a branch of the state. The reformed view has generally been that they are to be regarded as complementary and that, if the church is doing her job properly, the state might be made to tremble, as Mary Queen of Scots did as she listened to John Knox preaching. But there is no coercive power of the church over the state. The church has simply the power of the gospel and the authority of the Holy Spirit at the point of speaking to the state on moral and spiritual issues.

The principle I am stating is that we must recognize and respect the state for what it is. I go further. We must obey it. Here is the catch question, as put to our Lord. Should we render tribute to Caesar, or shouldn't we? The Herodians thought, "Now here is the point where we are going to get him. He is always talking about a kingdom. Of course, if he answers our question, he will have to say that he is not interested in the state at all. It is his kingdom that matters." They had, however, the surprise of their lives.

"Render unto Caesar," he replied, "the things that are Caesar's." He recognized the state as a divine ordinance. You must obey Caesar. You must pay your taxes. And remember, if you take that statement of the Lord's together with the statement of the apostle Paul in Romans 13 it meant this, that you must obey the state. Even if the emperor happens to be Nero, you still must obey it. You must keep its laws and be a law-abiding citizen. You do this as a matter of conscience, as the apostle teaches. You do it, in other words, as part of your obedience to God.

The state may not understand this. But every Christian should, and therefore he renders obedience to the state because God has ordained it. Therefore I, as a Christian, of all people, must render obedience to the state and its enactments. Indeed, the apostle Paul goes so far as to say that if you do not do it, but if you resist the state instead, you are resisting God. "Whosoever therefore resisteth the power, resisteth the ordinance of God: and they that resist shall receive to themselves damnation" (Rom. 13:2). Obviously, in the light of all this our business is to make the state as good as we can. It does not mean that we are content with an inefficient or unjust state. Because of the view we hold of it, it should be our object and ambition to make for the state the best working arrangement possible, and to do everything within our ability to bring about a righteous and prosperous condition of affairs that all "may lead a quiet and peaceable life in all godliness and honesty" (1 Tim. 2:2).

And, finally, as the apostle Paul did, we may claim the protection of the state. When he was told that he could go out from the prison, where he had been unjustly put, he replied, "Not at all! Let those magistrates come down." I am very fond of that passage. I can see those great magistrates having to slink down to let him out of the prison. We must not forget this sort of thing, or his appealing to Caesar.

Limits of cooperation with the state

Cooperation with the state has limits. First, the state has no right to become a despotism or a dictatorship, or to arrogate to itself absolute powers. Why? Because of what it is. It has been established under God and by his authority; it has no right to claim absolute powers. If, then, it sets itself up as a dictatorship, it is denying the law of its own being. It is showing an ignorance of its own constitution. It is going back upon that for which it was first brought into being. It is at this point that we have to question whether the time has not come for us to make a protest. It happened in Germany before the last war. There were men like Professor Karl Barth, who did not hesitate to speak out. They were speaking in a biblical manner. They said, "This is a violation of the very law and being of the state. This is dictatorship, this is despotism, it is unjustifiable in terms of the scriptural teaching." Therefore they opposed it, and were exiled or imprisoned.

Secondly, the state has never any right to ask a man to disobey God. It is for the same reason, for it is itself under God, in the same way that the church is under God. Of all the institutions, it has no right to ask a man to disobey God. Hence, the three young men of whom we read in Daniel who were thrown into the furnace rather than pray to a false god were absolutely right. They were asked by the state to disobey God's law. They said, "We will not do this." Daniel himself was put into the same position. The apostles in Acts 4 were told by the authorities not to preach any more in Christ's name. They said, "At this point we do not listen. Whether it is right that we should listen to you or unto God, judge ye." They then went on to say: "We know exactly where we stand. We cannot but speak of the things which we have seen and have heard."

Then, thirdly—and this is an important point—we have this old question of the interpretation of Revelation 13. The "beasts" represent, as most people would agree, the secular powers. The first "beast" undoubtedly represents the state and he is represented there as something that is entirely opposed to the Christian and his well-being. "How do you fit all that in," says someone, "with what you have just been saying about the state?" It seems to me, however, that the explanation is very simple. In Revelation 13 we have a picture of the state doing the very things that it should never do—becoming demonic. It is the state gone mad. It is the state deifying itself, and setting itself up as God, instead of recognizing that it is under God and serving the functions which God meant it to do. The picture is that of the state as it were, asking us to say, "Caesar is the Lord." It has no right to do so. Like the first Christians, we must reply, "We will never acknowledge that."

We say, "Jesus is Lord." If the state becomes demonic and religious and spiritual, then it has to be defied. I do not want to draw a red herring across at this point, but it is of interest to notice that some of the very Christian people on the Continent who courageously denounced Hitlerism have not denounced Communism in the same way. What has just been said is the reason for it. There is all the difference in the world between the state which is atheistical, or even anti-

God, and the state which become demonic and asks for worship and, in fact, becomes in itself a religion.

The Christian and strikes

This brings me to a practical question. Somebody may say: "What about a Christian and a strike? If a Christian is employed by the state should he come out on strike when called to do so? Where does that come in relation to all that you have said?" Let me put the answer like this.

I think we are in modern times face to face with certain new factors that are not dealt with specifically in the New Testament, because they were not then present. It does not make any difference to the principle. In the New Testament, employment was generally one of a simple direct relationship of master and servant, or owner and slave. That, however, is no longer the case, as we know very well. Very many are today employed by big companies or corporations or even by the state itself. Not only that, but we have the question and complication of the Trades Unions, which have become part of our social and economic milieu, and frequently enter into the terms of our employment. We have to recognize this. For instance, if I am a working man and I do not belong to a Trade Union, I cannot get a job. I am not allowed to work, and my wife and children will starve if I do not belong to a Trade Union. That has become a part of the terms of my employment. Negotiations between the Trade Union and the employer determine my whole position. This means that I must consider the Trade Union virtually as my employer. The position, though a little more complicated in essence, remains the same and, of course, it is legal. The state allows Trade Unions. Rather than negotiation by a series of individual interviews, it is more convenient that the workers should be organized and that their representatives should go to do the negotiating and that the bulk of the members abide by the decisions. Simple employment between master and servant is unusual today; a third party determines the conditions of employment. Further, there is nothing illegal about a strike as such. It is allowed by the law of the land, in certain circumstances and under certain conditions.

Christians have to recognize the condition of the world in which they live. We may need to become members of Trade Unions. We do so in the regular way, as everybody else does, to get our employment in order that we may have shelter, food and clothing, and we abide by the majority decision. Of course, we must in joining any union or other professional body try to make them as good and efficient as we can. We must not stay away from their meetings and let decisions be made only by non-Christians. We cannot make them Christian, but we can try to permeate them with good ideas. The Christian is in a perfectly legitimate position, when he belongs, if you like, to the British Medical Association or any other legal union. His representatives negotiate, certain decisions are arrived at, and he abides by these.

"Is there no situation," someone may ask, "in which a man may not object to his Union?" Certain situations may arise in which as a Christian he will have to say: "I object to this." He must be very sure, however, that his grounds of objection are truly Christian and spiritual. He must be sure that he is not being activated by some nonessential motive such as "professional dignity," or by his own political views, or merely by a matter of prejudice. A Christian is not meant to be a difficult or an angular person. If he is always objecting and walking out, it is a very bad testimony to Christ. If he makes a protest and objects then he must be certain that he has good scriptural and truly Christian grounds for so doing. As I see it a strike is not of necessity un-Christian.[2] In general we cannot say that. There might, however, be certain future circumstances in which we might need legitimately to take that view.

Applications to medicine and the National Health Service

Passing from this theoretical exposition of the Christian in relationship to the state, I must now briefly apply all this to medicine. I can be brief for this good reason that there is nothing, in these respects, very special about medicine. What is the difference in this matter between a policeman and a doctor? What is the difference between a postman and a doctor? People are talking as if this question of relationship with the state has never happened before, but it has been going on for many years. We have had medical civil servants, doctors in public health and doctors in government service overseas. The principles are exactly the same for all. That is why I have first taken all this time with the general principles.

In medical practice, we hear this sort of talk: "Medicine is no longer medicine"; "The profession is ruined"; "The doctor-patient relationship has gone forever"; and so on. Much of this is being pronounced as if it were a Christian viewpoint—as if we were bound to say it as Christians. But, while we would all agree that there are many defects in the National Health Service (and I am certainly not here to represent it or even to defend it) yet I still ask this question, is there not a great deal of confusion of principle at this point? When we talk about medicine being "ruined" and the doctor-patient relationship being "gone forever," are we really speaking as Christians? I wonder whether it is not just the pride of the profession? There is a lot of humbug talked about the professions—and perhaps, above all others, about the medical profession. A sort of "mystique" had developed in the nineteenth century. The "medical profession" had something indescribable about it, a kind of aura around it. It began when we were students. A medical student is different from other students, he is a special type, he knows a thing or two

94

which other people do not know. This unconscious attitude influences our thinking even as Christian people, and often when we think we are objecting as Christians, we are not doing so at all. We are objecting in terms of this great "mystique" of the medical profession.

Let us examine these complaints that "the patients are nowadays dictating to the doctors." I have no doubt that it is perfectly true. But there is another side even to that. There was a time when the doctors dictated to the patients. It may not perhaps be a bad thing that this state of affairs has come to an end. The profession had set itself up on a pedestal and in certain respects it really did tyrannize over the patients. I had learned a great deal about that by the time that I went into the ministry thirty years ago. It was a new experience, and a most illuminating one, to go into people's houses as a minister, and to discover what went on at the hands of the medical men. I came to know people who submitted to an operation for one reason only and that was they were afraid not to do so! They were afraid to offend their general practitioner and so possibly lose him as their family doctor. We have to look at both sides of this question. I have no doubt that some patients today are being unreasonable. They have the bit between their teeth, but it is perhaps a little bit of reaction against what went on before. But these considerations have nothing to do with Christianity.

Again, it is said that the Health Service is being abused by the doctors (by some doctors at least) who do the minimum. There is a town in which several doctors work. Before the Health Service they very rarely had a weekend off. They are now all working together; all but one is off duty each weekend and the odd man is left looking after the people. Supposing there is an emergency? Some will say, "Well, this is what the state scheme has done," and so on. To me, again, this has nothing to do with Christianity. All that this really tells us is that these men who are locally responsible may have had the

wrong motive in their work. It was possibly purely merce-
nary. They behaved as they did earlier because they would
have lost financially if they had not remained on duty. They
now have security and are behaving in a new way. It is not a
matter of Christianity or a lack of it. In other words, surely
the only big medical change is in the manner of the doctor's
remuneration. He is being paid in a different way, that is all. I
am putting it to you that such is the really big change that
has taken place. If you analyze all the other complaints, you
will find it very difficult to establish that they have got anything to do with Christianity. This one of pay is economic
and a matter purely of business organization.

The specifically Christian contribution

What is, then, the conclusion of the matter? The fundamental thing in the life of the Christian is his attitude to his work
and his attitude to whatever he is doing. This is, of course,
not confined to the medical profession. It is true of everybody
who works for the state. For instance, sometimes we have the
experience of meeting a polite girl serving behind the
counter of a busy store. Why? She may be a Christian, or at
least she has the right attitude. If she were a state employee
she should not say, "It does not matter how I do this work."
She takes the trouble to be pleasant and to be nice. It is her
attitude towards her work that determines her manner.
Surely, it is exactly the same with regard to the Christian
doctor and his work. A Christian man can never say, "Because I am paid by the state my action does not matter." If he
does talk like that, he is no longer behaving as a Christian.
He has a false standard. The Christian will say, "Everything I
do, I do to the glory of God." "Whether therefore ye eat, or
drink, or whatsoever ye do, do all to the glory of God" (1 Cor.
10:31). Ultimately he is not doing his work for the state, he is
doing it for God. He happens now to be paid by the state, but
his view of medicine should be exactly what his ideal for

medicine was before the state scheme came in. If he wanted to help that poor person who was suffering before, he should still want to do it. There may, of course, be pinpricks and difficulties which were not there before—though most of them were there in a different way. Centrally he is exactly where he was before. Consider the doctor-patient relationship. Why should the receipt of a check every month (instead of being paid by the patient there and then) make a difference to this relationship? A Christian will regard the patient as a soul, as a human being. Here is someone in trouble, who needs help. The best is given. That has always been done and is still being done. Where does the difference come?

Let me give you an illustration. Consider a man who was a grocer. He used to own his own grocer's shop. He was, of course, polite to his customers because the more polite he was the more customers he would have, the more they would buy and the more money he made. At a given point, however, a large store came along and said, "We want to buy you up." And they added, "We will not only buy you up, but we will leave you in the shop as manager." He eventually agrees. What would you think of that man if he says, "Well, course, it is no longer my shop. My salary is certain every Friday, whatever happens. It belongs to the big store, not to me," and he begins to be rude to his customers? Such a thing would be monstrous, wouldn't it? Why should the doctor have a different relationship to his patient and regard himself differently now, just because he is paid by the state instead of by the patients? What has it got to do with an essentially Christian attitude?

Let us notice the teaching of the apostle Paul in Colossians 3:22 and 23. "Servants," he says, "obey in all things your master according to the flesh; not with eyeservice, as menpleasers; but in singleness of heart, fearing God: and whatsoever ye do, do it heartily, as to the Lord, and not unto men." If we only keep such a consideration at the center, the whole problem, it seems to me, is not only simplified, but almost vanishes. We serve the Lord Christ. And we see in the light of that where the state comes into God's plan. Of course, there will be the annoyances. Yes, but does not that give us, as Christians, an exceptional opportunity to witness to our Lord? Here is a glorious opportunity for the Christian medical man. The older nurses of the hospital should be able to say of a staff doctor, "You know, he's exactly the same as he was before. I do not see any difference in his treatment of the patients." The family doctor's patients, who have known him all their lives, should be able to say the same thing. "This state scheme has not made any difference to our doctor." Why not? Because he is a Christian. He has his standards. He believes he has been called into this by God. He is serving God. He is serving the Lord Christ. So he overcomes the difficulties. And because he has this Christian view of his vocation, he goes on as before.

Of course, if a time should ever come when he is called upon by the state to kill off the disabled old people or to kill off the defective children or something like that, then he will take a stand and he will query the right of the state to arrogate to itself the control of life. But we certainly have not come to that yet. If we only view the total problem in the Christian way, we shall find that most of the difficulties will disappear. But if and when the states asks us to do something that is contrary to the commandment of God, we must then resist. We must refuse, whatever the cost. Until then we must recognize the true nature of the position and go forward doing our duty, not as unto men, but as unto God.

CHAPTER 7

The Making or Breaking of a Senior Resident: A Study of Stress

While we have been discussing these matters, I have reflected that these stresses are not confined to medicine. They are very common questions—I have had to spend most of my ministerial life in dealing with them. It is the plain fact that I generally have to listen to exactly the same sort of thing from ministers, ministerial students and people in other professions. So I think that you must abandon the notion that there is something peculiar to you, except in the sense that the particular phase through which medicine is passing has aggravated all these problems in your case. Hence, I think that a very helpful thing will be for all of you to realize, to quote the apostle Paul, that "there hath no temptation taken you but such as is common to man" (1 Cor. 10:13). Half of our troubles arise from the fact that we tend to think we are in some exceptional position and that we in particular have been dealt with unkindly or unfairly. The moment you think

From a paper which was one of a series of four given in turn by a physician, a surgeon, a psychiatrist and a minister and delivered before an audience of residents at the Royal Commonwealth Society, London, on Saturday, March 8, 1969.

like that you succumb. But we must realize that these are general problems which are common to all Christians and common to the whole of life simply because we are human beings and Christians in addition.

I have been listening carefully to the analysis of the stresses and strains as put forward by the representatives of three branches of the profession and also to the general discussion. I could not help feeling that the poor housewife, who is mother of a numerous family, could tell you something about stresses that would not only amaze you but would make you feel that you are really having a very good time! Take, for example, this question about pressures on your time. Think of the housewife with a house full of children! When is she to find the time to pray and to study the Scriptures? The children are constantly crying and screaming; first one falls, then another breaks a bone, while a third has tonsillitis. The husband comes home at six o'clock or later and expects attention rather than to lend his aid! This is something which a minister has to meet constantly, and there is nothing special about it all.

I would suggest that you are a little bit in danger, if I may diagnose you, of looking too much at yourselves and talking too much about your hard lot! So that I would say that the first bit of treatment which is needed is to make you realize that there is nothing peculiar about it—nothing special at all. Men in all professions are up against exactly the same thing. Take the matter of jealousy: look at politics or look at the bar! It even crops up in the ministry. It is everywhere.

Personal attitudes

Then, second, I would go on from there to borrow the words of Shakespeare: "The fault, dear Brutus, is not in our stars, but in ourselves that we are underlings." That quotation kept coming to me as I was listening. We moan about this wretched National Health Service. If only this were different, how wonderful we should be! We are not really being given a chance. Look at the kind of life which we have to live and look at those difficult chiefs under whom we have to serve and there is so much else wrong. But the answer is that "the fault, dear Brutus, is not in our stars. . . ." It is in ourselves. This again is a humbling realization. That is where the Christian message is of such help to us. It does not change the circumstances, but what it does is to change us.

It is at this point that we see the fallacy of the so-called social gospellers. They think that the business of Christianity is to change the environment, and to change the world. When everything is changed, we shall be all right! But this puts the gospel the wrong way round. The glory of our message is that circumstances, surroundings and "the stars" remain exactly as they are. We can, however, maintain our composure because our attitude is different. It is a change in us which enables us to view these things without—dare I say it?—having to go to consult a psychiatrist! We have to be careful in this matter because we have known of "psychiatrists" in the ministry who have spent a lifetime in preaching two main things: one, that a Christian, because he is properly integrated, will not suffer from insomnia, and secondly, that he will never have a nervous breakdown. Then these very advisers have proceeded to fall into both of these themselves! Apart from such uncertainties, it is bad Christianity. In fact, it is psychology, not Christianity.

The glory of the Christian position is that it puts us right. "If any man be in Christ, he is a new creature . . . all things are become new" (2 Cor. 5:17). Now, in what sense is this true? It is in the sense that he sees them differently. It is the secret of Christian life and of living.

> Two men look out through the same bars:
> One sees the mud, and one the stars.
> *F. Langbridge*

A primrose by a river's brim,
A yellow primrose was to him,
And it was nothing more.
                    W. Wordsworth

That's one kind of person. But, then "beauty is in the eye of the beholder." Another man can see beauty in "the meanest flower that blows," and have thoughts that often "lie too deep for tears." They are looking at the same things, but their reaction is entirely different. This is what the Christian faith should do for us—if we will only practice it.

The basic issue

Why are we then in trouble? Well, it is a case of, as our Lord put it, "If ye know these things, happy are ye if ye do them." To have an awareness of these things is not enough. So I would put it to you like this. The thing about which we have to keep on reminding ourselves, is that we are Christians. That is the big thing. In your case you are a Christian who happens to be a doctor. Another man is a Christian who happens to be called to the bar, or some other profession. But we must keep the fact that we are Christians always in the center. But, remember, this involves the necessity that you must keep on working out that principle.

I have observed over the years that there are many people who have broken down under these stresses because they have tended to live in "compartments." Yes, they are Christians. They are Christians in the sense that they read their Bible, pray and go to church. That is one side of them. But, then, when they go to their business they seem to forget all this, and in their work they are just like everybody else. They are subject to the same stresses and then they tend to break down and worry. I have known far too many Christians who seem to be two persons. At first you cannot tell whether they are Christians or not, then they suddenly pull themselves together and become serious. But I feel that there should be a unanimity about a Christian—a wholeness—which governs the whole of his life, his outlook and all his activities. To the extent that we are able to maintain that outlook, we shall evade many of the problems that we have been discussing together.

The pull of ambition

Then let us take the question of ambition which has been mentioned. There is nothing wrong with the desire to do well, as long as it does not master us. We must not be governed by ambition. There is a real difference at this point between the Christian and the non-Christian. The Christian starts with the realization that we are living in an evil world. The non-Christian does not have things in such a perspective. The New Testament repeatedly warns us against "the world." "Love not the world, neither the things that are in the world" (1 John 2:15); "The lust of the flesh, and the lust of the eyes, and the pride of life" (1 John 2:16). Yet I have known Christians who have been very worldly men. Not that they would be going every other night to a movie or a theater, or drinking heavily or gambling. But, in the matter of ostentation, for example in their houses and with their cars, they have been thoroughly worldly. They have not, of course, realized this, for "the pride of life" can be accepted in a very subtle form. I have also known many "snobbish" Christians. But this should be an impossibility! A Christian should never be a snob but I have known many who are. But that is wrong—it is of "the world."

The big thing that should be obvious about us is that we are Christians. "This is the victory that overcometh the world, even our faith" (1 John 5:4). So the Christian starts by seeing through "the world." He should, of course, want to be a good doctor. Given two men with equal ability, one a Christian and the other not, the Christian should be the better doctor of the two simply because he is a Christian. His whole attitude should be better and he should be anxious to function medically as perfectly as he can. Yet he is not a slave to good practice. Nor is he worried if somebody else is doing better. In other words, there is a difference between the desire to do your work well in order that you may have still more influence for good, and the worldly, unhealthy, totally self-centered type of ambition and pride which is the mark of the man of "the world."

I am, at this point, reminded of my old chief. I remember that he once asked me to go through the cards for his private patients. They had been indexed from their names. He wanted me to prepare a card index according to the patients' "diseases," so that if he were called upon to give a lecture on a given disease, he could at once lay his hands on the private cases of this. I went through all the cards of his private patients—thousands of them. I was most interested to see his diagnosis in the case of some, perhaps I should say many. He was a top consultant, yet his sole diagnosis for a number of them was—(a) "eats too much," (b) "drinks too much," (c) "dances too much," (d) "doesn't sleep enough." The Christian does not want to indulge or dissipate, hence he should be more efficient because he does not do so. The Christian is seeking to live his life to the glory of God.

As a result, it is not the end of the world for the Christian if he suddenly finds that he cannot go on to be a private consultant and has to go into general practice. He need not spend the rest of his life feeling a sense of grievance. Why not? Well, because he can equally serve God in general practice—perhaps better—and he can equally well do his best there. In other words, it is the higher and controlling attitude which saves the Christian from all these stresses and strains. But, it must be emphasized, he has to work this out quite deliberately. It will not happen automatically. It has to be worked out and it has to be applied all the time. A wrong thought may come to you, but you must confront and answer it in a Christian way. You may feel the risings of the old nature, which is still present. But it must not be allowed to control you.

Our temperaments

Then, let us look at this whole question of temperament. We all possess different temperaments, and we each have a personal problem for that reason. But the difference between the non-Christian and the Christian at this point is this: that the non-Christian tends to be governed by his temperament. Now, when we are converted and regenerated our temperament, as such, is not changed at all. It is still there and it should be. Christians are not intended to be all the same, like postage stamps. The apostle Paul was a violent persecutor before his conversion and he could be violent as a preacher afterwards. He was vehement as a persecutor and vehement as a preacher—that was his nature and that was not changed. The point is that the Christian is not controlled by his old nature. He controls it. He can harness it to become something very valuable because he will express his Christianity in his own particular way which is different from another. We all serve together to the glory of God. Just as there is a variety and variation in nature, so you have it in human beings and in Christians. We are not all meant to be exactly the same and doing exactly the same things. Such a consideration delivers a man from all the pettiness which is so often a characteristic of professional as well as ordinary life.

The futility of worry

The other big thing that you have to learn is this: you must not succumb to worry. It is bad, and, in any case, it is useless. Think of the time that we have all probably given to worrying about things. It is all a waste of energy. All you do is weaken yourself and hence become less efficient the next day. The

Christian should refuse to worry. You must face the cause, hold it up before you, and examine it. Then you must decisively reject it—"I know all about it; I am not going to worry, it is wrong."

But, then, on the positive side, there is the whole question of the nurture of the soul. This is something, of course, to which we all must attend. Medical men are in no special extremity in this matter. You would be surprised at the questions that ministers put in ministerial gatherings over the question of the use of time. I stayed recently with a busy minister and his great problem is that he is an artist. He has a real gift for painting. Should he give expression to this gift? If so, how much and how little? He was in a great frenzy over it. It will seem incredible to you but it is the bare truth that many ministers have to confess that their greatest problem today is to look after their own souls. Why? The chief reason is the multiplicity of meetings which they have. They are out every night in youth meetings, or meetings for this or that. Then people become ill and they must go round to visit them. They have no time properly to prepare their sermons. They no longer have time adequately to read their Bibles, nor to pray, yet remember that these are "full-time" Christian workers. I can assure you that they are confronted with exactly your own problem of time. This problem is not anything special or peculiar. There is only one answer, and it is self-discipline. Some of us expect things to come a little bit too easily.

A right perspective

I would suggest that you people are having a very good time! Do you know how much a house physician at a teaching hospital was paid in 1921? It was nothing! We could not think of getting married when we were students, nor as interns. We were unable to think of getting married even when we were residents. We just could not afford it, and we did not expect it. But, as a result of the last war, the idea came in that everybody is entitled to have everything at once. There is a lack of discipline, and though you are Christians you are being influenced by the mind and the outlook of the world.

There is only one answer to all this. The Christian must not be so self-centered and he must not indulge in self-pity. He must stop overprotecting himself. He has been given gifts. He did not create them. God has given him the gifts and his business is to use them—these particular gifts—to the glory of God. He is to do so with all his might and main. He can do no more. He commits his life to God and believes that God does guide, that God knows and loves his people. In that confidence he goes on and his relative position in life is to him not the big thing. If it is God's will that he should be in a commanding position, let him work honestly to get there. If he is not so meant, well, he is not unhappy. The apostle Paul has put all this in his picture of the church, as "the body of Christ" in 1 Corinthians 12. We have to grasp this notion that we are parts of the body of Christ, and wherever and whatever we are, we live to his glory. This is the essence, not only of the New Testament, but of Protestantism. The great discovery of Martin Luther was that a servant can brush a floor as much to the glory of God as any monk can pray in his cell. Everything we do is to be to the glory of God. We must become detached from self. Self is the subtle problem. It works itself out in self-pity, self-protection, self-concern, hypersensitivity, and the rest. Then come jealousy, envy, feeling grieved and hurt and all the rest of it. Christianity comes right to the center at once! You are to deny yourself, to take up the cross and to follow him. "He died for all, that they which live should not henceforth live unto themselves, but unto him which died for them, and rose again" (2 Cor. 5:15). If there is anything more glorious than this, then I would like to know what it is. The Christian faith delivers us from our wretched selves.

The vital attitude

The problems, of course, will be still there. But they will now be seen in a different way. It is your reaction to them that matters. It can be very difficult at times. Come back to your fundamental position, maintain your contact with God by your reading of the Scriptures and by prayer. You must make the time. As anyone may observe, you seem to have time for other things, so make sure that this comes first. Let other things wait, calm yourself, do not read your Bible in a hurry. Become quiet, get restful and be peaceful. Then study it because you enjoy it. You will then absorb the whole Christian "philosophy" and true outlook upon life.

I remembered a preacher some years ago telling us a story about William Wilberforce. I entirely disagreed with the point made then and still do. William Wilberforce at the height of the antislavery campaign was approached by a very pious lady who went to him and said: "Mr. Wilberforce, what about the soul?"

Wilberforce replied with great force, "Madam, I had almost forgotten that I had a soul."

The preacher seemed to think that this was marvellous! In the great campaign for the freedom of the slaves, Wilberforce had forgotten his own soul. But such a condition is quite wrong! It is a terrible thing that, however good the work you are doing, you should forget your own soul. The end of that course is often utter aridity. I have sometimes had to deal with those who have been active Christian workers all their lives and have seen them in the hospital or on their deathbed. They have awakened suddenly to the fact that they have been living on their activities and that their souls have been empty. They had failed to maintain the culture of their own souls. No work is so important that it must be done at the expense of your own soul. Keep your relationship with God right whatever else happens. If you keep that central, then I suggest to you that many of your problems, if not most of them, will certainly not break you. They will not even worry you.

Concentration on our tasks

It has been pathetic to me to see some good Christian men in the medical profession, as well as some in other professions, travelling about and preaching more than would seem to be wise. It raises the question of the doctor's task. Sometimes I have felt that all the activity has been due to the fact that these men have been uneasy in their own consciences. I have known some cases where I am quite sure that the trouble has been that the good man has felt that he should have gone out to the mission field. He did not do so and, then, as he began to do well in the profession, he sought to salve his conscience by preaching. But, in fact, you should know that a medial practitioner is not primarily called to preach. Let me tell you that! When I felt called upon to be a preacher, I left medicine. I became convinced that I was called upon first to be a preacher, and now and again, I practiced a little medicine. It is part of the muddle in the church today that everybody seems to be doing everybody else's job. I find that ministers in their training have now to do some psychiatry, and tend to become hybrid doctors, while some of the doctors are doing their preaching. We must stick to our appointed task. We must do what we are called, gifted and trained to do. Christian men have sometimes broken down in health simply because, in my opinion, they were killing themselves by doing the things for which they were never intended.

Maintain the culture of your soul. Never be so busy that you have no time for that. We are passing through a difficult time in every sphere, not only in medicine, but in the church. Everywhere this is the age of confusion. I feel that the call to all of us is to get back to the basic elementary things and to start again from there. This goes as much for the church as for the medical profession. We have got to get out of the present muddle. The only way to do that is for all to get back to first principles.

CHAPTER 8

Fullest Care

A new phrase has become increasingly common in current medical literature. We are reminded that we must no longer think in the old departmental terms, but that we must more and more learn to treat *"the whole man."* Yet this phrase may mean little or it may mean much. It depends upon its context and the occasion on which it is used. In the majority of instances, however, one fears that it is just one more expression of that loose and sentimental thinking which has become so characteristic of the present time.

The whole man

Let us look, for example, at this phrase "the whole man." How are we to define it? What do we mean by the word "whole"? The department of psychosomatic medicine has popularized the phrase but it has not adequately described it. Originally, at least, the phrase appears to have been intro-

From an address to a meeting of Christian doctors in 1957.

duced from Christian sources and notably from the literature of medical missions. But here again there does not seem to have been adequate thought given to the implications of the phrase nor to the alteration of meaning which occurred as soon as it was removed from its original setting. As soon as we look into the matter, the first surprise which must come to all of us is the realization of the ease with which we accept such phrases and build upon them, imagining that both we and those to whom we speak know precisely what is meant. In what follows, I wish to call for closer scrutiny of this phrase. I would also seriously suggest that, of all available sources, we have the best definition of it in the Christian gospels. Our Lord is constantly described as making those who came to him "perfectly whole" and the contexts in which such facts are recorded suggest that the statements were more than justified.

Psychosomatic medicine

I have not forgotten the fact that through articles in the medical journals, the profession as a whole has been made aware of much that it overlooked during the course of earlier developments of scientific research and its application in various forms of modern treatment. Most doctors, however little they may adjust themselves practically to it, make theoretical allowances for the subjective, psychological and the spiritual in treating their patients. Yet it would be premature to be too optimistic. For occasional stories from the outpatients' departments and also the wards of well known hospitals make it clear how easy it is for all of us to use appropriate phrases and neglect their obvious implications. The busy practitioner has scarcely been more then mildly interested, though in his case there are compensating factors. Fortunately, long experience of contact with suffering, interest in persons as persons, and the frequent necessity to take into consideration the situation of the whole family all unconsciously predispose to an adoption of the psychosomatic approach.

Yet when all is said and done, is psychosomatic medicine itself a fully adèquate response to what is basically required? Is it not itself another of those partial views which have been made to do duty for the whole? Is its application greatly in advance of the other attitudes which have done duty during the development of anthropology? Again and again definitions of the nature of man have been given which on further examination prove to be too narrowly based. The communist, for example, controlled by his philosophy of dialectical materialism, reduces man to a pawn of economics and politics. Other types of philosophy have isolated him as a piece of pure intellect, with the addition of a comforting doctrine that all he needs in order to emerge from his predicament is more and more education. Coming nearer home, the biologist concentrates on man's structure, abilities, movements, ductless glands and the functional balance of forces which enables the living organism to carry out an ordered existence. Even medicine itself is guilty of a very partial view. For over a hundred years morbid pathology has tended to dominate the picture, and while normal physiology has done something to redress the balance, yet in general the abnormal has come to distort the perspective. So now it is the turn of the advocates of the psychosomatic. "Yes," they say, "it is true that we have erred. We must cease to regard a patient as one who must be investigated like a biological specimen. We must take a bigger view. We must—in addition to our doctors and nurses—have cohorts of therapists trained in every form of assistance. We must treat *the whole man*."

But, even here again, are they not already tending to slip into the same error of falling short in their concept of man? When they have taken account, and rightly so, of all the subjective factors which may influence the condition of the patient, his psychology and the environment in which he lives

113

his life, is not their view still too limited? It cannot be emphasized too much that every view of man which omits from its consideration such a major factor as man's relationship with God, is doomed to partial measures. It can never fully and finally solve the crucial problem which lies at the root of humanity's unrest and "dis-ease." There is a major element in the very nature of man, which can be catered for in one way, and only in one way. As Augustine said: "Thou hast made us for Thyself, and our hearts are restless until they find their rest in Thee."

The bounds of medical practice

It therefore follows, if what we have so far said is true, that we must ask: can medicine in itself deal with the *whole* man? Can it as such, and by itself, ever do so? In any case, is it within the province of medicine to attempt such a thing? Is medicine able to function so as to ensure that mankind will function harmoniously in society? Is it able to reduce to order all those things which interfere with, and vitiate man's life? Surely, the practice of medicine was never intended nor equipped for such a function. Nor was it designed to uncover and to treat the evils gnawing at the heart of mankind. It cannot satisfy deep aspirations of the individual which are due to his very makeup and are accentuated by his estrangement from his Maker. Psychotherapy is no final answer. It may do much to help in restoring normal function to the mechanisms of the mind, but it cannot impart that positive addition for which each person's heart craves. Yet, without taking into consideration, and dealing with, such ultimate facts of human need, how can medicine possibly talk of treating "the whole man"?

I must here enter a strong caveat. Much loose thinking has come in at this point. I would without apology venture to make the blunt assertion that Christianity, and Christianity alone, can deal with "the whole man." By definition, it alone

114

is capable of undertaking such a task. Medicine is in its right place when it sets out to deal with the body and the mind. But it is the task of religion—of the Christian religion—to deal with "the whole man."

There are two processes at work today in the borderlands between medicine and the church. They are both clearly illustrated in Luke's description in Luke 17:12–19 of our Lord's healing of ten patients suffering from leprosy. Let us notice carefully the difference between the nine who failed to return thanks and the one who did so return. There was a vital difference in their whole outlook and attitude to the body-mind relationship. The group of nine patients were only interested in getting rid of the disease and its manifestations. Because of its signs on their bodies they had been ostracized and segregated from their people. As the record says, they "stood afar off." If they had done anything else than this they would have been severely punished. They longed— naturally they would do so, as any of us would—to be cured and to be able to go back into society. But their interest stopped at that point. They were only interested in getting rid of the symptoms and signs, so that they could return to their ordinary life and routine. They revealed no sign of wanting to be "made whole." On the other hand, the one who returned "with a loud voice glorified God," and the Master declared that this man's faith had made him "whole." In this particular case the man had not only lost the signs and symptoms of the serious disease that had been holding him in his grip, he had come into a new and right relationship with his Master. Of him it could now be truly said that he was made "whole."

Much of what one hears at the present time of certain "faith healing" movements illustrates the same two processes. The doctors of today are praised for their very wonderful discoveries and procedures. These have made an incredible difference in modern life and to the outlook of many who in past centuries would have suffered increasing disabilities or a slow decline to a fatal termination of their condition. But there are still numerous things which the doctors cannot manage. "Let us," many say, "go to the church and let us get as many people to pray for us as possible in the hope that somehow we shall be healed." But both patients and church continually forget the parable. These patients will go to God—they will go anywhere—in their anxiety as soon as possible to get rid of their diseases. But most of them at least do not seem to be in search of "wholeness"—that is in our Lord's meaning of the term. Their main anxiety is to get rid of their symptoms, signs of disease, and their immediate disabilities, so that they can speedily take their place again in society.

The place for Christianity

This matter of getting rid of symptoms, however, must never be mistaken for Christianity's essential function. Many members of the medical profession today, whatever lip service they may pay to it, simply regard Christianity as another specialty or another "therapy." When confronted with a particularly serious case with a bad prognosis, they will try all the therapies, radiotherapy, physiotherapy and, when these have all failed, at last they will say: "Ah, yes, it is really serious and beyond any help we can give—let us send him to the church and see what that department can do." But we must protest. Christianity is not just one extra, and final, link in a long chain of healing methods. It is not a branch of medicine. It never can be!

There is today a great deal of confusion at this point. There is with many an understandable (and, when it is rightly understood, commendable) desire for the closest cooperation between the profession which is responsible for caring for the body and that which is responsible for caring for the soul. Cooperation, if it is on the right basis of understanding and relative functioning of the partners in the enterprise, is, of course, valuable. If, however, the problem of a man's illness is to be undertaken in cooperation, then it will not do for the church to be regarded simply as a department of medicine. It is tempting to add at this point that it is certainly not for medicine to take over the church, but rather for the church to take over medicine! The church certainly cannot function simply as a branch of medicine. It must not come to be used simply as a means of getting rid of the more troublesome symptoms of mankind's divided heart and only that. Its essential value may thus be missed.

The church, also, is able to help medicine by fostering in its doctors, nurses and all concerned in treating disease some of the most needed virtues, for example, kindliness, patience, self-sacrificing service and much else. But when all such by-products have been supplied to medicine, we shall still not have arrived at treating "the whole man." In fact, if the church were to be prepared to let it go at that, it might be very misleading to the patient. It is dangerous to eliminate symptoms before the diagnosis has been assured. It is these symptoms which call attention to the presence and nature of the disease. Diagnosis becomes increasingly difficult if the symptoms are palliated too soon. The Christian faith must not allow itself to be used as a mere palliative. It may otherwise hide from the patient his real condition and prevent his arriving at a deeper understanding of his ultimate need.

There can be no real wholeness until each patient has come to a state comparable to that of the one man with leprosy who returned to our Lord and, "with a loud voice glorified God," that is, he really meant all he said. He fell at Christ's feet in adoration. He was both physically cured and spiritually restored. He was at last a whole man. He had been reconciled to God through our Lord Jesus Christ and had at last found peace. No man, by his very nature, can be finally satisfied until God fills his heart.

A final question

There is one further consideration, and we must not overlook or evade it. A man cannot with real composure face death and eternity apart from consciousness of reconciliation with his Maker. We all need peace with God. We are getting older. Some of the colleagues whom I see here today are those whom in earlier years I taught in our medical school. Speaking for myself, I can only face God in Jesus Christ, by spiritually dying and rising again in him, by being reconciled through him, and by living day by day in him. It is from him that I hear the liberating words, "Thy faith hath made thee whole." It is this spiritual element which ultimately matters to us. This goes on into eternity and, in Christ, I am ready for eternity.

Christian doctors, there is only one way in which we can really make men whole! Modern medicine has gained much for mankind and it may yet gain much more. But, when it has done its utmost it can only prolong man's life for a few more years. It cannot do more than repair a man's mind and body. It has to leave him there. It has nothing to say to the most vital element in man's nature. At this point Christianity alone can step in. When it does so, however, it can impart to the man something of incomparable worth. But before any of us can share it with others we must become Christians ourselves. Every doctor needs himself first to go to Christ. Then, with confidence, he can become a servant of the Lord of the New Testament who went about making men whole.

CHAPTER 9

Medicine in Modern Society

My only title to speak at all on this theme is my own past in the medical profession and my continuing interest in medicine. For the last forty years and more medicine has become my hobby, and I can assure you that it is a very interesting hobby. It's good to be able to look from the outside, as it were, on something concerning which you may have a modicum of knowledge.

But especially I am doing this because, though I am not in the profession now, I am still a great admirer of what I regard as the greatest of the professions. And as one who is concerned about the future of the profession, and especially its relationship to society, I avail myself of the opportunity of putting forward certain thoughts on the subject. The last thing I am going to do is give any advice. I believe that doctors are having much more than their share of such advice at the present time.

This talk was given in Wales in 1973 to members of the British Medical Association.

Changes in medicine: the role of the doctor

Now I want to emphasize this idea of the role of medicine in modern society. I put my emphasis on "modern," because I do not need to remind anyone of the amazing, quite astonishing change that has taken place, especially during the last forty years. One of the advantages of becoming old is that you can look back and compare and contrast the present scene with what once obtained. And I am old enough to remember the old idea of the doctor, the medical man. The man who was the guide, philosopher and friend to the family, who knew the family history with all its various happenings and circumstances. As for medical ethics at that time, it was comparatively simple. There were certain rules. The doctor must not advertise, he must not make advances to female patients, and he must not criticize his colleagues themselves or their treatment, at any rate not in public.

And so I still have this picture in my mind of a doctor entering a home, and it was quite an event. The tendency of the housewife, the mother of the family, at that time was almost to spring-clean the house when a doctor was going to pay a visit, he was such an important friend and was regarded with the highest respect possible. But a great change has taken place. A doctor once told me that quite often now when he does enter a house for a visit he finds that his visit is almost resented. The family are watching something on television, and he is an intrusion. They don't want to switch it off just to listen to what the doctor is going to say. It almost passes comprehension that such a change should take place. But many regard the doctor almost as their servant and he is subject to criticism. I noticed recently that even the Trade Unions ventured to express an opinion with regard to infamous conduct in a professional respect and I wondered whether the day would come when the medical profession would be controlled by trade union bosses.

However, this is the position. It is such a change that I find it extremely difficult to accommodate myself to it. For example, a book has appeared bearing the title, *Need Your Doctor be so Useless?* by Andrew Mollison, a medical man himself—I notice that he took the precaution of moving to Canada before he published his book. And then quite recently I read a book called *Complaints Against Doctors* by Rudolph Klein. Now the very fact that such a book has ever been published tells us a great deal about this change in the relationship between the doctor and the patient, or the doctor and the public; and I gathered from that book that it is a matter which is considered to be of the most urgent importance.

Why the relationship between doctor and patient has changed

So there we have the great change by which we are confronted and on which I base my remarks. I am going to approach this position first of all by considering the causes of it. For forty-six years I have been trying to shed medical thinking but I am a complete failure. I still have to approach every problem, whether it is theological or anything else, in this medical manner, and I start with the causes. What is the reason for this truly astounding change that has taken place in this relationship?

1. The National Health Service

First of all I would put the National Health Service, which came into being in 1948. That was truly a climactic point and things have not been the same since.[1] But it is not the only cause of the change and I really want to stress the other causes.

2. Advances in medicine

So I put second the very advances that have taken place in medicine itself. I believe they have been in a large measure responsible for this change in relationship. For instance, I re-

121

member the sulphonamides coming in, in the thirties, and then the antibiotics following. Again, there has been the extraordinary development in anesthesia, and, of course, this amazing development in psychopharmacology, whatever you may like to call it: psychotropic drugs, as well as stimulants—pep pills and so on. And then the tranquillizers; then the development of the hypnotic soporifics and so on. The antidepressants are surely an amazing development, equal in importance, I would have thought, to the coming of the antibiotics.

Then, in addition to that, we have had the physical treatment of mental and psychological troubles. That again, I hope to be able to show, has introduced a very important factor in the relationship between the doctor and the public. And then there is the surgery of the brain, lobotomy, and so on. And finally, of course, and more recently, the development of the transplanting of new organs into the body.

I suggest therefore that these advances in medicine itself have indeed played a very big part in this change in the doctor-patient relationship.

In addition, I would say that doctors, as I view them now from my position on the outside, have tended to become more and more technical. I seem to see a lessening of the old professional position and an increase in the technical element. This, of course, is a direct result of these phenomenal advances to which I have just been referring.

3. Public interest fed by half-truths from the media

Another factor in this changed relationship is the increased public interest in medical matters and in the behavior of medical men; there is a changed attitude on the part of the public. The press, for instance, has been daring to criticize and to give its opinion in articles by laymen, and the things that medical men do have been questioned and examined. And then we have TV medicine, which, were I given the powers of a dictator, I would prohibit completely, regarding it as extremely dangerous. I still remember an occasion when, as a very raw student, I was reading a textbook about pleurisy, and within half-an-hour I developed an acute attack—entirely mental of course, but it felt real enough. That is the kind of thing that you are asking for with this TV medicine. "A little learning is a dangerous thing," and especially, I would have thought, in the realm of medicine.

I travel a great deal these days, and talk to various people, staying with both doctors and lay people and I get the impression that the thalidomide case, too, has had a very profound effect upon this peculiar relationship between the doctor and the patient and the public. It made people think and question and examine. We have all read the articles, we have heard the discussions. I must try not to digress on this matter, but it seems to me to have been grossly unfair to doctors. But this is what happens when the public, with its lack of knowledge and information, ventures to express opinions on medical men and their works and their practice.

4. The permissive society

And then, of course, we are face to face with the permissive society in which we live, which has created new problems for the doctors that their forefathers certainly did not have to face. The permissiveness has led to great interest in birth control, the use of contraceptives and the desire for abortion. Now, these are new problems that have come in and, in my opinion, have had a very profound effect on the relationship between medicine and society.

5. Controversy between doctors

And the last factor which I suggest to you at this point concerns the conflicting evidence given by doctors in public law courts. This seems to have affected the public and has shaken their confidence. They find two men, of equal standing in the profession, disagreeing profoundly and completely with one another in their evidence in the public law court. This raises the question in the mind of certain members of the public as to whether either of them is really to be believed, and whether the whole idea of this charismatic personality, the doctor, was not a lot of rubbish, and that the doctor after all is more or less a very ordinary person.

These I think are the factors that have all conspired together. The result, as I see it, is that the doctor has less and more power, at one and the same time, than his predecessors used to have. I am afraid the mystique has gone. I think mystique is a good term for this charismatic person, the doctor, who came into the home, and was listened to and regarded by all as a kind of oracle. Now the mystique seems to have gone, and to that extent the doctor has less power, because that gave the doctor great authority. People were prepared to listen and to accept his verdict. But on the other hand I think the doctor has more independence than he used to have, and that has increased his power. As the technical aspect of medicine develops and increases, and the doctor becomes more and more of an expert, obviously his power will correspondingly increase because people will feel they do not know and therefore will have to be more dependent on him.

Consequences of the changed relationship

The issue to which I really want to direct attention is that of the dangers and the new problems that arise as a result of this changed position. Let me give you a number of headings.

Impersonality

The first consequence is the dangers and the problems that arise in the doctor-patient relationship which I am sure is less personal than it used to be. And there is an interesting paradox here. There has been more talk about what is called psychosomatic medicine than there was when I was practicing medicine fifty years ago. There is a new interest in the whole person, and not merely the local organ or the particular disease. One would have thought that that would, automatically, have led to a greater interest in the person as such. But it seems to have worked the other way around and one gets the impression that there is less personal interest in the patient than used to be the case.

The reasons for this fascinate me, and I have been trying to analyze them.

(a) *Antibiotics*. I have a feeling that antibiotics have been almost as important as the National Health Service itself in bringing about this lack of relationship between the doctor and the patient.

I still remember the days when a patient had pneumonia. You saw him propped up in bed, breathing rapidly, feverish and ill, in great trouble and you watched him. The doctor visited twice a day to see what was happening, what he could do, how he could medicate certain symptoms, and so on, waiting for this great crisis to develop. The doctor was in and out. He had to be. It was not that he could do very much, unfortunately, but nevertheless he was a great source of comfort and his visits had a great psychological effect. But above all it meant that there was this intense personal contact. But now, of course, when the patient gets a chill and a temperature the doctor is told this on the telephone. He asks the anxious relatives to send someone round to collect some tablets. These are collected, the antibiotics, or whatever they may be, and in a few days everything is quite all right, and the doctor may not have seen the patient at all. I suppose the subconscious argument is that if the tablets will do it there is no need to bother to go there. The tablets are going to have the desired effect and there is no need for the doctor to waste his time or energy in going to see the patient frequently.

(b) *Health clinics and group practices*. And then another

major factor is the development of clinics, and the tendency to get people to come to the clinic instead of visiting them in the home. Then there are group practices, of course. I am not necessarily criticizing these things, but merely mentioning them as factors which seem to me to have led to this loss of the personal interest between the doctor and the patient. The group practice means that you do not always see the same doctor as you used to, and if you happen to be living in London, and are taken ill at the weekend, it is very difficult to tell who you may see, if you see anybody at all.

(c) *Appointments secretaries and other intermediaries.* Then comparatively recently, as I have been observing it, there has been the appointment of secretaries, and appointments secretaries. This is a new factor. People have complained to me quite often that they are not able to speak to the doctor himself, as this person (I am sorry, they sometimes say, "this terrible person") answers the phone and says that there is no need for them to talk to the doctor. She can deal with the whole situation. And so the patient cannot make contact with the doctor, and is not allowed to ask questions, and is often not even allowed to speak to the doctor directly.

There is also a lack of information. The patient is not spoken to, is not told what the condition is and what is going to happen, in the way that used to be the case. There are these other persons coming between the doctor and the patient.

(d) *The deputizing service.* It is certainly very much the case in London, or any big city, that if you are ill at night, you will almost certainly not see your own doctor. Some appointed doctor, generally newly qualified and attached to a hospital, will come to see you, and I could tell some amusing stories in that respect. However, this situation again, I think, has worked in the same direction.

(e) *Specialization and experimentation.* Next I would mention the tendency to specialization, even among general practitioners. It may be a group practice, and one man is interested in children, another in geriatrics and another perhaps in midwifery and so on, and the tendency is for them to specialize among themselves. So all the cases with particular complaints go to one, and the others to another and so on. And on top of all this there is what I would call general overspecialization. I was very tempted when preparing this to take as my subject "Medicine, Art or Science," but I rejected it. However, I am simply mentioning now that I am afraid that science is winning the victory on all levels, for the more scientific medicine becomes, the less personal it will become, and the whole relationship between the doctor and the patient will deteriorate. The result is, with this ultrascientific attitude, that the patient becomes nothing but a case. Indeed when I was ill and had quite a big operation some years ago, I began to wonder whether I was a man or a test tube. All I heard was talk about input or output, the position of the potassium and the sodium and what was happening to the electrolytes. I began to wonder whether I was there, or whether I was just some curious test tube lying in a bed. And this is one of the dangers that is inevitable as medicine becomes more and more ultrascientific.

When you add to this what is known as clinical experimentation, which raises a very grave and important ethical and moral problem far too complex to discuss in a general lecture, I can say that the problems involved are very serious. It is all very well to say that you have received the patient's consent, but how many patients are in a position to give consent to some of these clinical experiments? They do not know and they are afraid to refuse any request that comes from a medical man. And the result, in my opinion, is that here we have a very serious problem which will have to be faced.

There, I think, are some of the factors with regard to this personal relationship. What have we to say about it? I think

that it is quite clear that the attacks upon us as human beings that come from the outside have in the main been mas-
tered and can be cured—I mean infections and such like
things. These can be dealt with by antibiotics and other rem-
edies. But increasingly, and this is to me what is so important, the real problem confronting medicine will be those
diseases that arise from the inside: the whole question of
stress and its related problems. We come again to psychosomatic medicine. Raised blood pressure, coronary trouble,
cancer and of course the psychological conditions are on the
increase and inevitably so, because of the pace of life and the
permissiveness that is so popular and which creates so many
problems.

Here is a field in which the medical man will have to exercise his skills more and more in the future. And I would argue that the personal approach will be paramount with these
particular diseases. With infection it is all right just to send
tablets—let an intelligent secretary even send them, or a
nurse who could soon be trained—but with these other conditions surely sympathy, understanding, reassurance and so
on are absolutely vital? The main point I am trying to make
is that the personal relationship will become increasingly
important as these two big groups of diseases and conditions
of ill health become more clearly delineated. However, I leave
it at that now.

The power of the doctor

Let me go on to a second group of problems and dangers
which it seems to me have arisen and will arise more and
more. And here I would describe it as the power of the doctor
as the result of the new knowledge, the drugs, the operations,
and the various other things to which I have referred. And
this surely is quite an alarming problem. The doctor today
has power not only to influence character and behavior, but
to change it by means of drugs, or by certain operations. I was

reading recently an excellent book by Professor Henry Miller, entitled *Medicine and Society*.[2] He quotes an eminent physician as saying that medicine is a social science, and politics nothing but medicine on a large scale. Now I think I understand what he meant by that, and what Henry Miller would mean by that. But I think it is a dangerous statement to make.

I also read a book recently called *The Politics of Therapy* by Seymour Halleck, an American psychiatrist.[3] He does not hesitate to go so far as to say that it is actually the duty of the therapist deliberately to influence the political opinions of the patient. He makes quite a thesis of this, and again it is very interesting reading. But here surely is a problem, and doctors will have to take it very seriously. I think their position is going to be extremely important in this matter.

Take for instance what we know to be happening in Russia, where men who dissent from the Communist philosophy and politics are not only thrown into prisons but are now being treated by doctors, so as to influence their conduct and their behavior. We hear that the same thing is happening in a measure in the United States of America; and I believe there is some ground for saying the same tendency has been noted even in this country. You may have read of a conference held by Amnesty International to consider this whole problem because of the terrible danger to individual liberty which has come about as the result of the discovery of these amazing drugs that can be used to influence personality. It is especially dangerous, of course, in a dictatorship, whether it be Communist or Fascist.

We have to face certain possibilities such as this: if you grant that it is right to use these drugs on any sort of agitator, any man who dissents from the accepted view, if it is considered to be right, if medical men can persuade themselves that they are even doing a kind of service to the patient in quietening him down a bit, then you might very well arrive at a position when you would never have another political reformer. Either the status quo would continue, or some dictatorship would continue, and it would be impossible ever to change it in any way whatsoever. If these drugs had been used in the past some of our greatest fellow countrymen would no doubt never have been heard of. Lloyd George would have been silenced immediately when he was a young attorney and fighting his cases, up against everybody. They would just have given him a tranquillizer or something, and that would have been the end of Lloyd George. But the point is that if this is done, any reform, surely, will become an utter impossibility.

Or take another very interesting problem. What are you going to do with the poets, because it is true, is it not, that much of the best poetry has come from rather unusual personalities, often men with a grudge against society? This is, you see, the genesis of poetry, this disease of unhappiness. The stories about the poets illustrate this quite clearly. They are often somewhat eccentric and they get their release by pouring out poetry. If you give them tranquillizers or antidepressants or anything else, they might be easier people to live with, but you would not have much great poetry. So this again is quite a serious possibility. If the doctor takes it upon himself to decide what kind of personality people should have, he puts himself into a position where he may put an end, nor only to great politics, but also to great poetry and great literature. So I think we need to consider these problems very seriously.

And then you have the whole idea of the possibility of genetic engineering, not only influencing those who have already been born, and are living, but even influencing those who are going to be born and producing some kind of standard type. I know this sounds like science fiction and I hope it will never happen. (I was pleased to read the distinguished Nobel Prize-winner Sir John Eccles' ridicule of the whole notion of this.) But nevertheless these are possibilities that seem to arise as a result of this phenomenal advance. Then there is also the whole issue of eugenics. The only lecture I ever heard in my life on eugenics was delivered in the library of St. Bartholomew's Hospital in London by the late Dean Inge. He was a strange looking man, and he was very near-sighted, with a high-pitched squeaky voice and one couldn't help wondering whether he would ever have come into existence if eugenics had been practiced in his youth.

The doctor as an authority

These are the points that arise almost inevitably. Now I want to come to a third danger. And this is the doctor as an authority, or as an expert. To me this is very serious again. It arises partly from the fact that certain medical men claim too much. They set themselves up as authorities, and speak with a dogmatism which, quite frequently, is not based on knowledge. And it is not only the fault of the doctors. So often a medical man who makes any kind of pronouncement is always referred to as an *expert*, and he is regarded as infallible. This is something that is resented, of course, in the realm of theology, since it is only popes who claim that kind of power and authority, yet it is what is often accorded to medical men because of their supposed superior knowledge.

Now the serious thing, to me, is the danger that arises from this view that certain medical men in particular are experts.

(a) *In politics.* Take, first of all, those who specialize in psychological matters. In *The Politics of Therapy*, Halleck says that American psychiatrists were polled by one of the weekly papers in 1964, as to whether one of the candidates in the Presidential election was emotionally fit to be President of the United States of America. A large number of them replied, and their answer went on record. The doctors had never examined the particular individual, but from just read-

131

ing his speeches and reading about him in the press, they took it upon themselves to make a pronouncement as to whether the man was emotionally fit or not to be President of the United States.

(b) *In punishment.* Then there is a great debate at the moment about giving evidence in a court of law. We have a mounting moral problem, juvenile delinquency, breakdown of morals, the increase in crime. But the question that arises is whether the action which the prisoner is being tried for is a disease or a crime. It is a most urgent question, especially with this new category of diminished responsibility. There are many who no longer believe in sin. There are many who do not even seem to believe in crime. Everything is a disease. And every delinquency can be explained in terms of diminished responsibility because of the patient's condition.

I speak with personal knowledge when I say that the influence of Freudianism in the Home Office is quite remarkable, and has been for a number of years. A lady once came to me who was in psychological trouble. She was rather an important person in the department in which she worked, and she had been more or less compelled to undergo deep analysis for two years in order that she might have experience of it, and thereby might be able to guide the people who were under her in that department. The effect of this deep analysis had been to create problems in that poor woman that had not existed before. And it took some time to get rid of them, one by one.

(c) *In education.* Again, take the effect and the influence of Freudian ideas upon our educational system, on our whole view of how children should be educated, and whether there is to be discipline and punishment. The influence of Freudianism, which has come, in the main, from medical men, has been quite astonishing.

And then we have our friend Dr. William Sargant, taking it upon himself to dismiss the whole of religion almost as an aside. I tried to answer his first book, *The Battle for the Mind*,[4] and now after reading his second book, *The Mind Possessed*, I am afraid I will have to try to answer this too. With his knowledge he claims he can dismiss religion, the Christian religion, and of course he affects the lives of many people.

The answer to all this is that more and more people are coming to see that Freud was never a scientist at all. The man was a poet, but he was taken to be a scientist because he claimed to be one. His teaching was swallowed whole, without any discrimination, and it has had this almost devastating effect in many homes during the last fifty years or so. I wish I had the power to make everybody read Jung, and Jung's criticisms of Freud and his reasons for departing from Freud and his school. However, in any case, there is a real danger here, it seems to me, where the doctor speaks dogmatically as an expert.

(d) *In ethics*. Lastly I come to some ethical and moral matters. The doctor is regarded as the authority in the matter of contraception, abortion, homosexuality, euthanasia, and sometimes just maintaining existence—not life but just keeping life going. The patient has really ceased to be. He is reduced to a kind of test tube existence, and the doctor keeps him there. These are some of the problems that are arising acutely.

I was reading an article by Professor Robert Veatch in the *Harvard Theological Journal*, entitled: "Medical Ethics, Professional or Universal." His great point was what he called the generalization of expertise, which he illustrated in this way. Would we, he asked, dream of calling upon the U.S. Defense Department nuclear bomb experts to decide whether or not to bomb an enemy country? Now, these men are experts on bombs. Would we, because of this, go to them for an opinion as to whether we should bomb another country, simply because they are experts on bombs? Then he quoted, rather aptly, a physician in America who said that an abortion is no more a medical question than capital punishment through electrocution is a problem in electrical engineering —a rather profound statement. Your electrical engineer is an expert in his field. Do you ask him, therefore, to decide whether a man should be electrocuted? Of course not! A doctor has expertise in birth and all the problems connected with the birth of a child. Does that entitle him to be the authority who gives the final opinion on the rightness or wrongness of abortion? I agree with Professor Veatch. In fact, this is a great fallacy. It is the problem of technical knowledge versus judgements and these two things are very different.

These problems which I have mentioned—contraception, abortion, euthanasia and the rest of them—are not really medical problems but theological problems pure and simple. They are moral, ethical and ultimately theological. What decides these issues is your view of man and of life, your view of death, your opinion about what may or may not happen after death.

So the medical man, because of his expertise, must be very careful here. His danger is of course to impose his own ideas, moral, ethical and, yes, let me say it, even Christian—upon his patient, and he has no right to do so. No man has a right to impose his own personal views on the patient. Because of this relationship between doctor and patient, the patient, on the whole, is ready to listen and the danger then is that the doctor will tyrannize the patient. I have always said to Christian medical men that they must not foist their opinions upon their patients. They are being bad doctors if they do so. Certainly give an opinion if asked for it, but at the same time a doctor must ultimately have the right to refuse to do something that is definitely against his conscience, whatever it may chance to be.

This is a difficult knife edge. All I am trying to say is that the doctor must be very careful that he does not take an unfair advantage of the position, and that he does not make the tragic blunder of confusing his expertise with his moral, his ethical, and his value judgements.

The general practitioner: my plea

What then is to be the role of medicine in modern society? Here, surely, the great thing is to have a balanced view.

Neither a dictator nor a slave

The doctor must not be a dictator. Professor Veatch again says that professional paternalism which negates individual freedom in favor of professional decision-making is rejected by an ethic which is applicable to all humanity. But although the doctor must not be a dictator, neither must he be a slave, or a mere servant of the public. It seems to me that many people today are thinking of their doctors in much the same way as did certain Eastern potentates. These men would have great banquets, and at a given point in the banquet a slave would come along with a kind of balloon at the end of a stick and would proceed to hit the back of the ears of this great emperor or potentate with the balloon. In this way he was actually stimulating "James's nerve" (you remember) in order to improve the great man's digestion!

Now it seems to me that many people are regarding their doctors now more or less as the slave who tickled "James's nerve." What is a doctor? Well, he is a man who gives you certificates, he is a man who give you pills. His patients issue their demands and he is expected to deliver the goods immediately, and if he does not, a complaint will be registered. This surely is quite wrong. I am afraid this lack of balance is due to an increasing failure to realize the true greatness of the profession.

A man who respects the medical profession

I read an article recently in *Modern Medicine,* the first article by the chairman of the Patients' Association. She says there that one of her people had told her that he had sent for a doctor in the middle of the night and the reply the doctor had given was: "I don't call out the plumber or my solicitor or my accountant in the middle of the night, so why should I turn out?"

I think that is really tragic. That is surely a case for the General Medical Council; it is infinitely worse than infamous conduct. I do not care how bad the morals of a doctor may be—I would forgive him a great deal—but when a man has that view of the medical profession, putting it into the category of the plumber, the solicitor and the accountant, he cannot see the uniqueness of this profession. Here is a man coming to people in an hour of need and of crisis, when they are troubled, ill and unhappy, and the whole family is involved in this. And yet this doctor clearly fails to realize that he is in this extraordinarily privileged position, because the doctor becomes increasingly important as the church is ignored. People no longer go to places of worship, nor do they consult their ministers. They go to the doctor; to whom else can they go? And this greatly enhances his privileged position in society.

What then, in my humble opinion, is the greatest need? I do not hesitate to say this: it is for great general practitioners. This is my plea. I read somewhere the other day a statement to this effect. General practice, says the writer, will remain a dangerous mixture of twentieth century science and medieval witchcraft! With great risk I venture to put in a plea for the "medieval witchcraft"! Very well, go on with your twentieth century science, but do not forget what he calls the "witchcraft," which I have called the "mystique," the "charisma," of the doctor. I put in a plea for a new order, for a new conception, of general practitioners and in addition general consultants also. As a young man I worked for some six years with Lord Horder. He was a general consultant. He was not a specialist in any one department. He was a general consultant, and that, I think, was the genius, the great value of the man.

A watchdog and guide

So, then, what is the general practitioner to do? What is the general consultant to do? I would say that his main function is to keep an eye on the experts, on the specialists. Have you heard Marshall McLuhan's definition of a specialist? He says that a specialist is one who never makes a small mistake while moving towards the grand fallacy. He never makes small mistakes. But what about the grand fallacy! So that is the first business of the general practitioner—to keep his eye on the expert. He does not finish with his patient when he sends him to the expert. Follow him on, keep an eye on him, help the patient to decide. It is a terrible thing for a poor patient to have to decide whether or not to have an operation advised by the specialist. The general practitioner is to be there, by his side, and to help him. And he is to keep an eye on the treatment of the whole man, when the specialist tends to look at only one part of the man. What are the guiding principles?

A man of humility

The first great need is humility. The greatest danger of all as a result of this phenomenal advance in medicine is for medical men to claim too much, to speak beyond their knowledge, to speak beyond their right to speak. I notice increasingly the humility of the great Nobel Prize-winners. What do we really know about the brain? We talk about manipulating it, changing it, affecting it. What do we know about mind? What do we really know about either of these?

137

And the answer is—very little. And yet people play with these new drugs with impunity, not realizing that they are going well beyond the knowledge which they possess.

A man of humanity

Remember the great Hippocratic principle: do no harm? Do the patient no harm. But I want to go beyond that and put it in a positive form. Do unto others what you would have others do unto you. It is a very good test. If you are confronted by the question of one of these clinical experiments, look at it in that way. Would you like to have this catheter pushed down your veins and into your heart? Would you like it to be done to you? Above all, be concerned for people as people. Be concerned for the whole man. Never was there greater need for character in medical men—understanding, sympathy and patience. Yes, and self-sacrifice.

The doctor of the future

I would like to see a new order of general practitioners coming into being, men who have a sense of vocation, who are aware of a call, men who are prepared to be counsellors, in a general sense. They can send off these patients to the specialists and the experts as the need arises, but they still maintain their hold of them. The patient can still go back to them because they are always in charge. Surely this ought to appeal to many young men today. The doctor in the community. I believe his is, in many ways, going to be the guardian of personal liberty. He alone I think can do it, because everybody will turn to him because of his expertise. I think personal liberty may well be in the hands of general practitioners of this type in the years that lie ahead, and it would be a wonderful thing if a body of men, an order of men, emerged holding this high exalted view of the general practitioner in society and in his community, serving the public. I would pay him well, more than he has ever asked for, in order to encourage him to give himself in this way to helping his fellow men and women.

What is my prognosis, then, with regard to the future? I believe that after the upheaval through which we have gone in the last thirty years or so, medicine will settle down again. We will see that we have reached the probability of no further advance, and then we will be able to sift all this, and to take a more balanced view of it. And medicine, I think, will settle down again into a happier condition than it has been in during the last thirty years. All this, of course, if the experts and the technicians, as a result of their brilliant advances in knowledge, but with their corresponding failure to advance in wisdom, have not succeeded in destroying themselves and us and the whole of civilization in the immediate future.

Such are my ruminations about medicine in modern society. Some of you, no doubt, have been amused at the obvious conflict that has been going on between the lecturer and the preacher, while others have diagnosed an obvious case of schizophrenia! Well, whatever your diagnosis, all I say is that as one who has a profound respect for this great profession, I hope I have been able to convey to you this one idea, that there is still a paramount need of those ideas and motives and thoughts which moved and impelled a man called Rahere to found St. Bartholomew's Hospital in 1123.

CHAPTER 10

Body, Mind and Spirit

Introduction

I feel it is a very great privilege, indeed a great honor, to be asked to give this lecture, and that for a number of reasons. One is that I had the pleasure of knowing Professor Rendle Short quite well. In our student days he was one of those men who were known as "a Christian doctor." By now this is a fairly common term. But thirty, forty or fifty years ago it was rather uncommon. There were, however, two men, Rendle Short in this country and Dr. Howard Kelly in the United States of America, who in religious circles were so known. This tells us a good deal about Rendle Short. He was a distinguished surgeon and widely known for his writings, but pre-eminently he stood out as "a Christian doctor."

So it is very right that there should be this annual lectureship to commemorate him and his great work.

I could not help wondering, however, as I was preparing this lecture, how far he himself would actually be interested in the subject on which I intend to speak. He was primarily in-

This talk was given as the Rendle Short Memorial Lecture for 1974.

terested in the relationship between the Christian faith, science and the rest of life in a realistic manner. Most of his Christian writings were concerning various aspects of apologetics. He took a very objective view. That, I believe, was not only due to the fact that he was a surgeon, but still more, I think, to the religious denomination (or absence of denomination) to which he happened to belong. Its members are characterized by this objectivity rather than by a more subjective approach, which is more characteristic of the various branches of Methodism. So I do not know how interested he would be in what I am going to attempt in this lecture and my approach to the subject I have chosen—"Body, Mind and Spirit."

Let me at once make it clear that I am not proposing to give a theological lecture on the nature of man, and the vexed question whether he is to be viewed as bipartite or tripartite. I am rather going to consider with you some of the perplexing problems—extremely difficult problems—which confront both medical practitioners and ministers of religion because, after all, we are all of us "body, mind and spirit"; and these have a complex interrelationship in different aspects of our being. In other words, I want to consider with you those patients who come either to the doctor or the minister because they are in trouble and are unhappy for a variety of possible reasons. They may be depressed, or worried about something, or oppressed by certain fears. They may be worried about the question of God's forgiveness, or lack of assurance about their standing before God. They may be unable to concentrate on their work and, in extreme cases, begin to show suicidal tendencies. The spectrum of particular symptoms is a very wide one indeed.

Now we are seeing an increasing number of such cases at the present time. I believe that this is due to several factors. It is partly due to the hectic character and pace of modern life, and all the stresses and strains of modern work situations.

My reason for calling attention to it is that I for one have certainly had to spend a great deal of time trying to help in such cases. I have been so often asked to talk about it, because I believe it is a fact that there is no competent textbook which deals with this need. At least I am not aware of one. It is the field where the physical, the psychological, the spiritual and the psychic tend to meet.

At this point I must also make it clear that I intend to confine attention in this lecture to Christians who are in trouble in these respects. It would be impossible in the time at my disposal also to take in the wide field of the experience of non-Christians.

Some general considerations for doctors

Let me at the onset make a number of general remarks. The first is that we need to pay much more attention than we have done to this whole subject. There are, indeed, several available books which approach the situation, such as those of Dr. Paul Tournier, and that enormous treatise on *Clinical Theology* by Dr. Frank Lake.[1] But I feel that there is more to be said in this particular area. My own interest has been constantly stimulated not only from personal experience of such cases, but by constant requests from ministers of religion and doctors to speak on it.

Now I believe that in the near future medical men are going to become increasingly important in this sphere, largely because of the regrettable general decline of the church and the Christian faith. Not so many ministers are available and people therefore are driven to seek such help from the doctor. Yet there is a very curious factor which disturbs me considerably. That is, that although in medicine there is a great deal of talk about the "psychosomatic," the personal element and "the medicine of the whole person," a great deal of it seems to me only a matter of lip service. Going about the country my observations suggest that the practice of medicine is becom-

143

ing increasingly impersonal, and one hears of an increased reluctance of doctors to visit patients in their homes.

There are, of course, numerous reasons for this. We need not go into them, except to mention, for example, antibiotics* and the National Health Service. There is, however, no doubt that—compounded by the increased clinical loads on the practitioner as a result of the sheer numbers served by the NHS—there is less, and more fleeting, contact between the average doctor and patient. Yet there never was a greater need of such intimate personal contact and knowledge than there is in today's circumstances.

Then I have observed a number of faulty attitudes on the part of some medical men. This is especially true of the surgeons, who tend to dismiss these patients entirely as "neurotics." The surgical attitude towards them tends to be that all they need is a little breezy reassurance, a slap on the back and advice to take more exercise. I am going to show you that this is a totally inadequate approach. As is also that of the practitioner (or physician) who contents himself with prescribing tablets of some sort and trying to calm the patient, while resigning himself to the prospect of having to anticipate periodic visits, where he will just repeat the dose. In this way he never really meets the actual situation as it needs to be met. From a strictly medical point of view this process may not seem to be very serious, but I hope to show that in daily life, and to the unfortunate sufferers, it may be very serious indeed.

The difficulties for a minister

In the case of ministers of religion, when they are consulted by these persons, there are also several dangers. One is that a minister may tend to get too involved. That is very rarely the danger of the medical man. He has learned to be more

*Cf. lecture on Medicine in Modern Society, Chapter 9.

detached—he has to be—and to develop a kind of protective mechanism in order to retain due objectivity. But the minister, with less experience of this type of consultation, is apt to become too emotionally involved in his efforts to sympathize. I have known a number of instances where ministers have really been brought almost to a breakdown themselves in their efforts to identify themselves with the difficulties of members of their congregations.

Another danger for a minister is to regard each case as spiritual and to approach it wholly on spiritual lines. I have frequently told the story of how, on returning to Westminster Chapel late on Sunday afternoon, I was followed into the vestry by two excellent members of the congregation. They looked pale, drawn and completely exhausted. On asking what was the matter they told me that they had been talking to a man for three hours. They had not made the slightest difference to him and had only succeeded in exhausting themselves. He proved to be a manic depressive, who had had repeated treatments in various institutions. They had been trying to deal with him purely in a spiritual manner.

A further difficulty for ministers in these aspects of their work is that some patients feel that they cannot trust the minister, because they are afraid that they may be used as illustrations from the pulpit. Some years back, for example, I became acquainted with an American minister who came on a visit to Britain because, he said, he was on "the verge of a breakdown" and the deacons of his church insisted on six months' rest and sent him on a holiday. During a Sunday morning service in one of the churches in England something had been said which had completely solved his problem. When he told me this story I commented, "Well, surely you could have consulted one of your minister friends in America? Did you go and talk to them?"

"Oh no," he said, "I was afraid to."

When I asked him why, he replied, "I would have been used

145

as an illustration in a sermon. They would not have mentioned my name, but they would have given so many details that most people would have been able to work it out and discover that I was the man." The ministry's overuse of illustrations discouraged this man from going to those who were most in a position to help.

These are general dangers, but there is one particular aspect of this matter to which I must refer and which amazed me some thirty-five years ago. Evangelical churches at the time had been much opposed to psychology until then. For example, on the whole they had frowned on a well known minister of religion, who was also a psychologist and who wrote books on the usefulness of psychology in the work of the ministry. Then suddenly psychology came into vogue and in these circles they were sending people with any difficulties to see a psychologist. At that time I had a young man come to see me one Sunday evening in a very worried state and asking if I could recommend "a Christian psychologist." On enquiring why, he explained that he was an evangelist and had been advised to go to a certain college for training. But, because of inadequate earlier education, he had found it very difficult to follow the lectures. On going to the principal to explain this he was immediately advised, "You must see a psychologist."

This trend became a widespread vogue and several psychologists—most Freudians—developed an extensive clinical psychology practice. One heard even of missionary societies sending their candidates to be interviewed by a psychologist (or psychotherapist) in order to find whether they were fit people to be sent to the mission fields. Such procedures, of course, were being followed in business and other fields. But it was truly astonishing to find that the fashion had begun to invade evangelical circles.

My last general remark is that lay Christians seem to me to do untold harm to this kind of sufferer. Almost invariably I have to spend time undoing what some overzealous lay person has done by talking in a somewhat glib manner with a number of cliches and generalizations. This not only has not helped, but often done much more harm than good.

Physical illness

I am going to approach the problem by describing as best I can my own practice over the years. For example, sometimes after a service I would be standing in my vestry, when someone would come in. It would be clear that this person was in some kind of trouble. What was I to do to help? Well, the first task was always diagnosis. To what group, or department, did they belong—in other words, what was the differential diagnosis? And this is really my theme in this lecture—the differential diagnosis of the distressed people who may come to you with their problems. Let me say at once, it is something that is extremely difficult. I find that differential diagnosis in this realm is usually much more difficult than in clinical medicine—difficult as that may be at times. It is a vast subject. I cannot pretend to deal with it exhaustively, but I will offer some basic points.

The trouble with attempting to deal with this is that it is easier to carry out in practice than to state in words what the process really is. I do not mean that the essential work is done by some sort of instinct or horse sense, though an element of this may come into it. Experience, too, is valuable. But it is a complicated process. One has to make evaluations and estimates. So much depends also on question and answer. I have tried to put all this into words for years and still find it extremely difficult. Yet what I am trying to describe is something very essential. For I have known persons who have been treated in a very cruel manner. Those responsible for this were not aware of it, did not wish to be cruel and were only so because of their ignorance. We are dealing with souls, with persons. We are all sensitive and in a sense highly

147

strung and finely balanced. Great harm can be done without due care.

Very well, here before us is a patient, or a person who is seeking our help, or what today is called "counselling." How do we start? The first question I always ask myself is, "Is it *physical*?" I wish to emphasize this, because there are some to whom it never occurs that the whole cause may be physical. Because the complaint is regarded as "nervous" it is at once assumed that there cannot be a physical cause. But frequently this has proved to be the case.

On one occasion when I was to preach both afternoon and evening in a certain town, I was asked between the services to see a schoolmistress who had become intensely depressed and unhappy. She had given up her superintendency of the Sunday school and had become irregular in her church attendance. She was having treatment by correspondence from a well known minister, who also practiced clinical psychology. I took one look and noticed the lemon yellow of pernicious anemia (which today would—I hope—have been treated much earlier). The treatment of the anemia soon put that woman right.

I remember another instance—and I am giving you these examples to make my meaning quite clear. I had been asked to see an old man who was bedridden, and I was told that he was "swearing like a trooper." He had been a highly respected deacon of a local chapel, but here he was puzzling everyone with the problem of where he had learned this new vocabulary. The old man's behavior was puzzling his poor wife, his relatives, the minister and the doctor with whom I saw him. He proved to be suffering from advanced arteriosclerosis, no doubt with considerable involvement of the cerebral arteries. I was able to explain to the great relief of the relatives that this was not a spiritual, but a *physical*, problem.

This point is very interesting and has recently been raised in the medical press in relation to the illness of King George

III. Research into the medical features appears to suggest that his periodic bouts of madness can quite simply be explained by the fact that he was suffering from porphyria. Another example is the great Charles Haddon Spurgeon. He used to have periodic fits of depression, when he felt he was not called to preach and sometimes that he was not even fit to preach. What was the matter with him? Well, he suffered from gout, and if you have the gouty diathesis (and have it in the particular form which he had) you *will* at times be depressed! It is part of the condition. One, therefore, needs to start with the possibility that any given case may have a physical cause.

Now I have a particularly interesting case to add to the above. It concerns Charles Darwin. The facts were given by Max Hammerton, a Cambridge experimental psychologist during a discussion in a BBC program entitled "Freud: the status of an illusion." He says, "During much of Darwin's long life he suffered from a mysterious illness characterized by heart palpitations and feelings of lethargy and gloom. His doctors could discern no physical cause and, as he himself suspected and rather resented, he was believed to be a hypochondriac.

"Darwin's hypochondria was a gift to the postmortem analysts (that is, Freud and company) and how they spread themselves over it! Darwin, they explained, hated his father. 'How did they know?' you will ask. Well, they say so. Besides, 'He once wrote that his father was the kindest man he had ever known, and that proves it'—and they add 'doesn't it?' So he hated his father and felt guilty about it. Also, they say, he felt that his theories had 'dethroned God,' who was a sort of heavenly Father. This made Darwin's life work 'symbolically equivalent to killing or castrating his father,' which he wanted to do anyway (Oedipus and all that). He felt guilty about it. So, having a powerful conscience ('super-ego' is the word in their jargon) he proceeded to punish himself with psychosomatic illness and misery.

"I have to spoil this lovely fantasy," says Hammerton, "by pointing out that none of it is called for, because it now appears that Darwin had contracted Chagas' disease during his stay in Argentina, and the symptoms of Chagas' disease, which is a kind of parasitic infection, are palpitations, lethargy and gloom!"

I have turned up Chagas' disease, of which I had never heard before, and find that the symptoms described in recent textbooks bear those characteristics.

Here was a man labelled as being neurotic and as suffering from psychosomatic illness, whereas the whole explanation was a physical and natural one. In 1956 I remember that I stumbled across a book in America with a most arresting title. It was, *Body, Mind and Sugar.* It was written by a medical man and biochemist on hyperinsulinemia. The case seemed established beyond doubt. The experimenters gave their patients a dose of glucose and then took the blood sugars every hour. The thesis of the book was that, if you took the blood sugar at the sixth hour after the glucose dose, it would give indications of hyperinsulinemia (the exact opposite of diabetes). The number of symptoms that this condition can produce mentally—mental nervous symptoms—are really quite astonishing.

I hope I have emphasized sufficiently the importance of excluding at the outset a possible or conceivable physical cause.

Spiritual illness

The second question I ask myself is this: "If it is not physical, is it spiritual?" (Let me digress here to say that this was the order I adopted until comparatively recently, but I might now vary it a little. However, let me adhere to my practice through the years.) What do I mean by a spiritual problem? It is one which can be dealt with entirely in spiritual terms. For example, the commonest problem is lack of assurance. Many are troubled about this. Others are concerned about some particular sin and how they can be rid of it. Or it may be the memory of a particular sin, or of an incident of blasphemy, or sin against the Holy Spirit, or some serious lapse in conduct.

It is important to be aware that such "spiritual" cases can come with "presenting symptoms" which may be quite alarming. I will give a striking illustration. One day some years ago I was told that there was a man at the door in a state of great agitation, accompanied by a younger man. I went to the door and there was a tall fellow, with his hair all ruffled, in a very great state of agitation, who could scarcely contain himself. I brought them into my study and began to talk. I found that this man had just discharged himself from a nursing home, where he had been treated six weeks for "religious mania." He was desperate, virtually tearing his hair. When in his desperation he took hold of me I had the terrible feeling that he could crush me if he wanted to.

The story was that this man had been converted in the Welsh Revival of 1904–5. He had been delivered from drunkenness and became an active Christian. Partly as a result of the change he began to prosper in business. But after some years he began to grow somewhat careless and spiritual decline began to set in. He started to drink again with friends and to become a thoroughgoing backslider. He had gone on like this for some years, outwardly doing very well for himself and certainly becoming a wealthy man. Then, suddenly and without warning, the reality of his position had come home to him. He began to worry about it deeply. He began to accuse himself in the following way. "Of course, before, when I was unconverted and I did these things, I did not know any better and I was forgiven. But now, I have sinned against the light. While living as I have recently been, I knew the truth and knew better—and now there is no forgiveness."

The doctor had diagnosed him as suffering from religious mania and he had been put in the nursing home, where he became worse rather than better.[2]

The treatment which I gave this man was purely spiritual. There was no need to have known any medicine at all. I dealt with him purely in terms of the teaching of Scripture. He was completely delivered. I have had many other such cases, one of which will suffice.

A lady in a quite prominent and responsible position, which involved her taking prayers each morning, had got herself into a state where she could no longer do this. At first she would sweat violently on each occasion and, at last, she could no longer do what was required. It was all because of something she had said about God twenty-two years before. She had had two courses of deep analysis, both, I think, by the psychologist mentioned earlier. I received a letter asking if I would see her. But she only had one question for me, "Could I recommend to her a Christian psychologist." It was a request which I frequently met when I was the minister of Westminster Chapel. This was all she wanted.

I replied—"But why do you need to see a psychologist?" (That is the essential question to put on frequent occasions.)

She then told me her story. It was clear that she needed a proper understanding of the Scriptures and of the nature of God. She was completely delivered, is still alive and rejoicing in her active Christian life.

It will be clear to you that the important point is a diagnostic one. I have always found that with persons in this spiritual category there is a clear diagnostic point. They always show a readiness to listen and they almost jump at any of the verses quoted which give them relief. They hold on to what will really bring comfort and release. One must not be put off by their appearing at first to demur a little, with a, "Yes, but . . ." They are really doing this in the hope that you can go on to make your case still stronger. They *want* you to make your case and in my experience it is a diagnostic pointer to those in this group.

Psychological illness

The third category to which your patient, or enquirer, may belong is the psychological. I use that general term, but if you prefer it, it could be "mental illness." This is at the present time an important consideration because we are now in the midst of one of the latest crazes, or fashions, in the Christian, and even evangelical, world. The concept of "mental illness" has come under attack at the present time, mainly as the result of the writings of Thomas Szasz. He has written a number of books such as *The Myth of Mental Illness, The Manufacture of Madness, Ideology and Insanity*.

What is Szasz's thesis? He contends that this regarding of people as mentally ill, and treating them accordingly, is but the latest manifestation of something which has taken place for centuries. In the Middle Ages, he claims, it was the punishment of heterodoxy by the church. A heretic was ostracized and punished in various ways by the Inquisition. This gradually passed out of fashion and was replaced by witch hunting, and this latter lasted until the end of the seventeenth century in this country and in America. What do they do now? Szasz's reply is, "they diagnose people as being mentally ill and put them in various institutions." The argument is that this is precisely what is happening and that it is something we have to resist.

This man Szasz and his writings are not only interesting, but entertaining. He is a brilliant writer and an able man. If you want some enjoyable reading you should sample some of his books, which are available, for example, in the library of the Royal Society of Medicine and may have been imported, or printed, in Britain by now. There is a good deal of truth in what he says. He is an anti-Freudian and he is attacking what has become a cult—"Send him to a psychologist." Everyone is labelled and everything is covered by the psychological. Szasz discusses the financial aspects of this—and it needs to be dealt with. But what concerns him still more is the element of moral judgement that is involved. Sometimes a man becomes labelled in a moral sense by his wife, family and the doctor. He may be completely helpless and he is simply handed over to treatment in some form. He is assessed, judgements are passed on him and if this process continues and becomes more prevalent there will be an acute danger to individual liberty.

The press, from time to time, gives glimpses of what—in an extreme form—is happening in Russia. But there is no doubt at all that in America some of the same sort of thing in a polite form has entered a lot into industry. Men fail to get a post, or are sacked, on such pyschologists' categorizations. People who are in any way different may find themselves labelled, a judgement will be passed and they will be manipulated in spite of their wishes. Szasz is concerned to point out how these psychologists (or sometimes even psychiatrists) take it upon themselves to pass sweeping opinions. Everyone can be explained—Hamlet, for example, or Darwin, as indicated above. But this trend is not simply confined to a few postmortem diagnoses. The writer quotes a case of a man setting up to run for election as President of the U.S.A. who was assessed in this way. The report was published in the newspapers, and there were people ready to believe it and to regard these psychologists as having a complete understanding of human nature and the characteristics and foibles of any given individual.

So Szasz emphasizes the tremendous danger. What he is out to prove is that you read what they did with people considered "mad" in the past, and you are horrified; but, he urges, they are doing exactly the same now in a more polite way. In his book *The Manufacture of Madness* he point out,

As recently as 1860 it was not necessary to be mentally ill to be incarcerated in a maniacal mental institution. It was enough to be a married woman! When the celebrated Mrs. Packard was hospitalized in Jacksonville State Insane Asylum for disagreeing with her minister husband, the commitment laws of the State of Illinois were such that married women could be entered or detained in the hospital at the request of her husband or guardian, without the usual evidence of insanity required in other cases!

This woman was thrown into an asylum for venturing to disagree with her "minister husband"![3]

What is your reaction to such a statement? I am sure that most of you would bemoan the fact that human beings could ever have been guilty of such conduct. (Though one or two present may be muttering to themselves, "*Those* were the days!") However, I am convinced that Szasz completely overstates his case. While there is a considerable element of truth in much that he says, he goes too far in saying that there is no such thing as mental illness. Unfortunately, too, he now has a number of followers who are writing up his views in popular books. One of the best know is Jay Adams with his widely selling *Competent to Counsel*. But he is just a popularizer of Thomas Szasz and he is simply affirming, with Szasz, that there is no such entity as mental illness, that the patients are really suffering from sin and need to be dealt with purely in a scriptural manner. These writers reprimand those sufferers and counsel them with great severity.

It is necessary for us to work with those in this field who have to establish the reality of mental illness, otherwise we are going to be guilty of great cruelty to some of those who come to consult us. Why would I affirm the reality of such illness? I suggest that the familiar (hereditary) element in the case histories alone is sufficient to establish it. Another factor is the periodicity so characteristic of many cases—clear,

155

lucid intervals, and then a recurrence. Not only that, but there are many cases of mental illness which do not respond at all to spiritual, scriptural treatment and, indeed, are even made worse by this.

I would argue along the following lines. There are various psychological types. Some persons are placid, some are mercurial and others are temperamentally different. In mental illness these variations are carried further as disease entities. It is, at least, becoming more popular today to take the view that mental illness results from defects in the chemistry of the brain, just as diabetes results from derangement of the chemistry of the pancreas. Difficult as it may be to classify them, there are obviously some clear clinical entities in mental medicine.

In history there have been cases which clearly establish the fact of mental illness. One that is outstanding is William Cowper the poet. He was a dedicated Christian man, who knew evangelical doctrine and delighted in it. But he had periodic attacks of his mental condition. His friends reasoned with him, and did all that we are often told we should do to help our cases, but without result. It rather made him worse and added to his distress.

A Puritan writer of three hundred years ago—Richard Baxter—in a most remarkable manner reveals great insight at this point. Baxter, better than anyone I have ever read on this subject, provides us with the differential diagnosis between a spiritual and a mental case. He says,

> I do not call those melancholy who are rationally sorrowful for sin, and sensible of this misery, and solicitous about their recovery and salvation, though it be with as great seriousness as the faculties can bear. As long as they have sound reason, and the imagination, fantasy or thinking faculty is not crazed or diseased. But by *melancholy* [i.e. mental illness] I mean this diseased craziness, hurt or error of the imagination, and consequently of the understanding, which is known by these signs.

156

He then gives thirty-five points in the differential diagnosis between what may be called "mentally ill" cases as distinct from those who are in "spiritual" distress. The following are some of the points he makes concerning those mentally ill:

(i)   They are commonly exceedingly fearful, causelessly or beyond what there is cause for. Everything which they hear is ready to increase their fears, especially if fear was the first cause, as ordinarily it is.

(ii) Their fantasy acts most in aggravating their sin or dangers or unhappiness.

(iii) They are still addicted to excess of sadness, some weeping they know not why, and some thinking it ought to be so, and if they should smile or speak merrily their hearts smite them, for it is as if they had done amiss.

(iv) They place most of their religion in sorrowing and austerities to the flesh.

(v)   They are continually self-accusers, turning all into matter of accusation against themselves, which they hear or read or see or think of.

(vi) They are still apprehending themselves forsaken of God and are prone to despair.

(vii) They are still thinking that the day of grace is past and that it is now too late to repent or to find mercy.

(viii) They are oft tempted to gather despairing thoughts from the doctrine of Predestination, and to think that if God had reprobated them or had not elected them, all they can do, or that the world can do, cannot save them.

And on he goes with his list of thirty-five points. But he ends in the following way:

Point 35. Yet in all this distemper, few of them will believe that they are melancholy [melancholic, or mentally disturbed], but abhor to hear men tell them so, and say it is but the rational sense of their unhappiness, and for the forsakings and heavy wrath of God. And therefore they are hardly persuaded to take any physic or use any means for the cure of their bodies, saying they are well, and being confident that it is only their souls that are distressed. This is the miserable case of these poor people greatly to be pitied, and not to be despised by any. I have spoken nothing but what I have often seen and known, and let none despise such, for men of all sorts do fall into this misery, learned and unlearned, high and low, good and bad; yea some that have lived in greatest jollity and sensuality when God hath made them feel their folly.

I cannot add to that. I do hope that people who tend to follow Thomas Szasz and his popularizer Jay Adams will take all that to heart.

As far as my own experience would go, I would summarize Baxter's thirty-five points in the following way: I think that you will find almost invariably that those who are mentally ill do not really listen to you. You quote Scripture, they do not listen. They keep repeating the same statements and give the impression that they are waiting for you to finish so that they can say their piece over again. This is almost invariable. You notice the difference as compared with those in spiritual trouble. The latter are anxious to have help. The others are not. I always feel with them that I am a kind of tangent to a circle. One never penetrates, they are almost impatient and go on repeating the same thing.

Demonic oppression

This brings us to my last category which is "the demonic." Am I confronted in this case with the physical or the spiritual or the psychological or the truly "demonic"? Now here again, I feel that I must defend the category I am putting before you, because it is disputed. It has always been disputed, of course, by non-Christians, by unbelievers; for they do not believe in the spiritual realm at all. The difficulty is that many Christians do not seem to believe in it either. The author, Jay Adams, to whose *Competent to Counsel* I referred earlier, in another book (under some title such as *Under the Broad Umbrella*) says quite specifically that demon possession has not taken place since the apostolic era, and cannot take place any more; and therefore it is not even to be considered as a possibility when dealing with this kind of case.

This seems to me to be very serious indeed, and it has relevance to ourselves, for I have known evangelical Christians who take this same view. It was taken also by B. B. Warfield and those of his school. They say that spiritual gifts and similar manifestations—such as miracles and speaking in "tongues"—came to an end in the apostolic era and so demon possession came to an end at the same time. This seems to me not only dangerous, but to be completely unscriptural. They have no warrant for saying that baptism with the Spirit, or the giving of spiritual gifts, ended with the apostolic era. There is no scriptural evidence for that whatsoever. In the same way, there is no scriptural evidence for saying that the manifestations of demon activity—the activity of evil spirits—ended at that time.

The moment you begin to say *that*, then the question I would ask you is—"How much of the New Testament do you believe? How much do you believe is relevant to us today?" When Paul says, "We wrestle not against flesh and blood, but against principalities, against powers . . ." (Eph. 6:12), was this only for the Christians of the first century? Has it nothing to say to us? I suggest that in this attitude we have a new and very dangerous form of dispensationalism. Still more important and serious is the fact that, in my experience, what appears to me to be the results of demonic activity is a very, very common cause of people's coming to see the minister, and, also, to a lesser extent, to some of you in general practice.

Demonic activity is on the increase. What is the reason? Well, I would say that primarily it is due to the lowered spirituality, and the godlessness of the whole country. There is always a kind of hangover after a great period of spiritual revival. The influence continues for several generations. This country has been living on the capital of the Evangelical Awakening of the eighteenth century for nearly two centuries. I believe we have come to the end of it. It was for long a restraining influence, as were the smaller revivals of the nineteenth century. But the influence has now gone. As godlessness increases, and the whole concept of God in the public mind diminishes, you would expect a corresponding increase in manifestations of the evil forces. Another factor is drug taking, which knocks out the higher centers of control and the ability to discriminate, and leaves the victims a prey to the influence of the evil forces round about us.

Another factor is the increased amount of dabbling in the occult in various forms. There have been recent reports of the involvement of school children. Many cases have been reported in the Greater London area in recent years, and it can be a very great problem. Then there are the popular and widespread hysterical agencies today, such as pop music. This primitive type of music and rhythmic movement appeals to the lower instincts. It weakens or removes the higher controls altogether and makes people more obvious prey to the unseen powers around and about them.

Lastly, I must mention the so-called charismatic movement, or rather, not the movement as such, but those people who are always so subject to crazes and fashions that they go headlong into them. Rather than "trying" or "testing the spirits" they abandon themselves to anything which will give them a new experience. It is an age which is crying out for experience. We are witnessing a revolt against "reason." People are tired of reason, "Where does it bring you?" they ask, and they go in search of an experience. This is why they begin to sample drugs and other things. It is such factors which explain the increasingly common problem of demonic activity.

I would divide the contemporary phenomena of the demonic kind into two groups. There is first what may be called demon "oppression." It is oppression—not depression (or "possession"), although there may seem little difference between oppression and depression. I would prefer to call such cases "satanic attacks." There is an immense literature concerning the lives of the saints in church history which gives what seem to be authenticated examples of oppression from satanic sources. I believe that examples are becoming increasingly common today.

Let me give one or two examples. I was asked to see a man who had been appointed a minister of a church. His history was that he had joined that church when living in the locality, while serving as a secretary to a society. He was a good Christian and, though he had not received the fullest education, he had very effectively stood in for any of the absences of the minister. On such occasions he always preached with great acceptance. When the minister of this church received a call to another church and left, the elders agreed that they need not look far for a successor and unanimously invited this man to succeed. He accepted the call. But from that moment he began to be seriously depressed, which was a state that he had never known before. He became so depressed that he could not even face the welcome service at the church.

When I saw him, I found that he had been in this condition for thirteen months, and during all that time he had not once preached in the church which had given him a unanimous call. He had not only been treated by the local general practitioner but by a distinguished psychiatrist, who was a personal friend of that practitioner. The patient was very proud of this, and mentioned the fact that the specialist had given him his home telephone number in case he should be so acutely in trouble that he would like to telephone—thereby telling me that he had had suicidal tendencies. He had had almost every known form of treatment for the condition, but had grown steadily worse. When he came to see me he was a picture of melancholy, and it was distressing to look at him. On another occasion, too, I was brought into contact with yet another minister who suddenly found that he could not preach.

But perhaps a more striking case was that of a qualified nurse who had gone to one of the republics of South America and done what was clearly a wonderful work among the Indians. She was a very able girl, and when the superintendent, and only surgeon, at the hospital for these primitive people was compelled by illness to take a long furlough back in Britain, she had been able to maintain a considerable proportion of the services. On the surgeon's return he at once arranged for her to go on furlough, and after a period of rest she engaged in deputation journeys for her Society. While staying with her sister in London she was introduced to a girl needing help. The girl's mother was a spiritist and the excellent and successful missionary began to help her, and saw her several times. Then, quite suddenly, this missionary became depressed. Whereas she had been champing at the bit to get back to the mission hospital, now she did not wish to go back and felt that she was not fit to go. She came into a most unhappy condition. I have found that this type of case is commonest amongst ministers, missionaries and evangelists, who have seemed to have been welcomed and successful in their work.

I am suggesting that each of these cases came under the category of "oppression"—demonic oppression. This brings me to the diagnostic points. What are they? First, the sudden onset of the condition; second, it was something unexpected in this type of person, and something that they had never had before. Suddenly these excellent people are changed and become more or less useless. There is always a suggestion of an occult opposition to the work of God which they are doing, as if an enemy is out to spoil or stop it.

As I listened to the story of the man who received a call to the church but could not preach (literally for thirteen months) I had to ask myself whether this was really a psychiatric case. Was it not rather a matter of direct satanic opposition? All the while he was filling in for the minister things were wonderful, and hence the congregation had given the call. The devil then seemed to say to him, "Who are you to be the minister of a church? It is all very well to preach on an occasional Sunday, almost anyone can do that, and most lay preachers fool themselves because of it. But is another matter to preach every Sunday, morning and evening, Sunday after Sunday—and there are well educated and professional men in the congregation and you have never been to college . . . It is all very well to preach for one Sunday . . . !"

Incidentally, one must always let such people talk freely. I allowed this man to talk for an hour and, the more he said, the more I was sure of the diagnosis. When he had finished I began to say, "Look here, you are no more mentally ill than I am."

He resented this and explained, "I have been treated by this great specialist."

I replied, "Yes, I know you have, but I am telling you that you are not mentally ill at all."

"Well, what is the matter with me?"

I said, "You have been oppressed by the devil."

He really did not like this—he was a medical patient and he urged that he had been given all this treatment. He had, however, brought his wife with him. She had been present throughout and I saw that I had convinced her. So she turned to him and said, "Don't you remember that the last time we saw the doctor, he said to us, 'I don't understand you at all. According to all the rules, that combination of drugs which I

163

gave you last time ought to have made you very much better, I do not understand it.'"

"Well I do understand it," I said.

At this, he asked somewhat aggressively, "What is your understanding?"

I replied, "My understanding is this, that every conceivable combination and permutation of drugs has not the slightest effect on the devil!" That registered and I saw that I had gone home. In another twenty minutes that man was not only relaxed but I had got him to smile. I told him that he must start preaching immediately, which he did.

Some five or six weeks later I was just leaving the house when the phone went and I answered it. It was this man who said, "You remember that I told you that our church had had three or four whole nights of prayer for my recovery?"

"Yes," I said, "quite well."

"I thought you would like to know that we are having an all-night prayer meeting tonight to thank God for my recovery."

The only "treatment" which I gave was to show him that he was not mentally ill, but that the devil—who knew he was going to have a good ministry—was trying to keep him out of that pulpit. That is what I mean by recognizing the element of opposition to God's work involved in such a case.

Another diagnostic element is extreme weakness. There was a case of a minister, a very strong, muscular and hefty fellow, who, when I had arrived to preach at his church, said, "Do you see the mailbox down the road? When I went to post some letters there the other afternoon, it took me all my time to drag myself home in a state of exhaustion. Sometimes I have found it almost impossible to lift up a knife and fork because of extreme weakness."

There was a similar case of a minister in Liverpool who was sent back three times to a hospital for investigation of the state of his pancreas, and search for other possible explanations of his extreme debility. All the finds were negative. One spiritual talk not only rid that man of all his symptoms, but he continued strongly with his ministry.

Another excellent minister, not a highly intellectual one, but one who had to preach to a number of well-educated and highly intellectual people, began to feel that he was inadequate. The devil's insinuations—"the fiery darts of the wicked" as Paul would term them—would come as he awoke in the morning. This is another diagnostic point—in such cases the moment that they wake in the morning these thoughts fill their minds and blight their day.

Then the last diagnostic point is that they, of course, make no response to any medical treatment, no matter what it is. They also baffle all those who treat them medically or psychiatrically.

Demon possession

Then there are the cases which can only be regarded as demon possession. Several books have been written which deal with this serious matter very well. For example, there is that excellent booklet *The Roaring Lion*, published by the Overseas Missionary Fellowship.[4] I commend it to you, it is very instructive. Then there is the popular book *From Witchcraft to Christ*.[5] I have come across several cases in my own experience.

What are the diagnostic points in these cases? You generally find a history of dabbling with spiritualism or the occult in some form. It may have been back in their childhood, or during teenage, that they have been introduced to the occult and experimented with occult phenomena. They may also have experimented with drugs.

One clear diagnostic point is that one becomes aware of a dual personality. There is another person. You see it in the face, hear it in the voice. It is an unnatural and quite different voice and can very often be accompanied by horrifying facial expressions. There is also—a most important point—an alteration between what we may call a normal and an abnormal element. These persons can be one moment quite normal and can discuss things quite readily for a time; then suddenly they change. The "other" person seems to take charge. They will tell you that they are conscious of suggestions and voices; and frequently that they have come to have abnormal powers. In my experience there was a woman who was able to hold a complete conversation with a man in Swedish, a language of which she had never learned a word.

A still more significant pointer is their reaction to the name of our Lord. I always tell ministers who are confronted by the duty of treating such cases to use the phrase—"Jesus Christ is come in the flesh" and to note the reaction. Talk to them of "the blood of Christ" and you will generally find that they will react quite violently to this.

On one occasion when I was visiting a certain town to preach, the minister and elders of the church told me of their experience with a local girl who had been "possessed." It is important here to add that she was a Christian. Christians in certain circumstances may become possessed. In this lecture I am talking of Christians. If we open the doors to evil powers we can be possessed by them. Christians will often reply: "But how can anyone who is filled with the Holy Spirit be possessed?" But this is because they are thinking of the Holy Spirit as if he were a liquid. Popular, but dubious, illustrations are often used, such as that a vessel must be emptied in order to be filled and so on. But this is all wrong, the Holy Spirit is a person. We must yield ourselves to his rule and direction and give no opportunity to any evil power. My point, however, here, is to emphasize the way in which this type of case reacts.

I had earlier on the phone advised this minister and his elders that they should (after first praying for themselves, and for our Lord's protection from evil) go to this girl and explain to her: "In our opinion you are being tormented and possessed by an evil spirit, would you like to be free?" If she said "Yes," that they should pray for her, repeatedly using the phrase, "Jesus Christ is come in the flesh." They must then be prepared for the likely antagonistic action. They had done as I had advised and they were now reporting the result. They said that as they were praying, one of their number used the phrase advised. The girl reacted in a horrifying voice and shouted, "Jesus Christ is *not* come in the flesh" and went down on all fours and began to bark like a dog. This had given them the assurance that they were on the right lines and they prayed all the more earnestly for her deliverance. Then one of them in Christ's name commanded the spirit to leave her. She then became quite quiet and said in a calm voice, "He's gone." I had the joy of seeing her in the evening service with her face radiant, as we sang the closing hymn, "Jesu, Lover of My Soul."

I remember, when I myself was dealing with such a case that when I used that phrase about the Lord the woman began to shout in the most unearthly voice I have ever heard! Again, she went down on hands and knees and made noises in a similar manner, until she grew quiet and was delivered from the possession. She remained free.

Types of approach in treatment

I have left too little time for what I wished to say on a few points about treatment. If a case is physical, then, of course, you will treat it in accordance with the best medical standards. If it is demonic the choice of the correct treatment is not difficult. There is nothing that one do but to seek the divine aid for the exorcism of the evil spirit. There is, as you know, a Church of England service of exorcism. The late Bishop of Exeter has produced a booklet which, in my opinion, explains this very well indeed. It teaches clearly what should be done and not done. Similarly, if it is a case of oppression—and I do not hesitate to say this—you will always be able to deliver them by reasoning with them out of the Scriptures. I do not mean by just quoting Scripture but deploying the whole basic arguments of Scripture concerning salvation, calling and service.

But I want to say more about those in the psychosomatic category. A psychosomatic case needs particular proof. It is of no use to give general reassurance. For example, if a patient is convinced that he has a cancer of the bowel, or any other organ, he will not take your word for it that he is not so afflicted. You can waste a lot of your time and theirs. They need proof from the appropriate examinations and the radiology department. Show them the X-rays and given them maximum proof.

Similarly if dealing with "spiritual" cases there is a need of detailed proof. What I mean here is, that one must be precise and detailed in bringing to bear the scriptural arguments. The impression that one can just pat them on the back and tell them "Don't worry" is not only wrong, it can be real cruelty. We need to be very patient. We may need to go over the same arguments more than once. There may need to be a number of visits, but you must keep on and on. The same applies to some of the cases of demonic oppression. You must "reason out of the Scriptures," which means that you must know your Scriptures, know the relevant verses and know where to find them. They will say, "Where is that in the Bible?" and, if you do not know, half of your influence has gone. You must know your case, demonstrate it and produce your evidence.

What of the mental cases? I can but refer to a few points. I could say a lot about Freudianism, which I personally believe we should not touch. I shall have to deal with it on some other occasion. At any rate we can now thank God that today it seems that Freudianism is obviously, and we trust, rapidly, on the way out. Again, I am equally sure that the application of surgery in this field of mental disease is never legitimate; and I was delighted, recently, to see reports of a symposium in which several leading psychiatrists and surgeons, who had formerly advocated lobotomy, stated quite openly that they would never do it again.

Religious experience and drugs

There is one other difficulty which might be noticed. What are we to say to those Christians who assert that it is sinful to take drugs? Here I am sure that the answer is that it is no more sinful to take drugs to put right the chemistry of the brain, than it is to substitute for the abnormal chemistry of the pancreas in a diabetic case by the use of insulin. If it is right to use insulin in replacement therapy for the pancreas, why is it wrong to take tablets which influence for good the chemistry of the brain? I think we must get hold of the concept that mental illness is really something that has an "organic" basis. It is something that can be explained chemically. We have all been so unconsciously conditioned by Freudian ideas that we must now try to get rid of them. We must hope that the future here lies with progress in clinical pharmacology.

But, when we have convinced some people that it is not sinful to take drugs, we are confronted by a new problem. There are those who ask, "Do not the taking of drugs and the experiences which they give rise to, undermine the whole concept of salvation and explain away the divine providence and intervention?"

Here again there is a complete answer. R. C. Zaehner, who was Professor of Eastern Religion and Ethics in Oxford, wrote *Drugs, Mysticism and Make-Believe*,[6] in which he proves beyond doubt that the effects of drugs and mystical states rarely overlap. He shows that the experiences of those who are under the influence of LSD are not at all the same thing as types of religious experience. He goes into great detail, ad-

169

duces clear evidence and reports what other similar literature has confirmed.

Another book—a very remarkable book—was published in 1973 by John Bowker (a Fellow of Corpus Christi College, Cambridge) entitled *The Sense of God*.[7] It is a difficult book, but a very important one. In a chapter on "The Physiology of the Brain and Claims to Religious Experience," he answers this question very convincingly. His thesis is that what these drugs are doing is to release something which is already there. They do not give rise to anything new; all they do is to release thought processes and concepts already in the mind. The fact that under the influence of a drug, some people may simulate the religious experiences and concepts which resemble those reported in times of religious revivals, does not prove anything about the being of God or the validity of any religious experience.

The same applies to the work and writings of the psychiatrist Dr. William Sargant. In a way his whole thesis is rather pathetic. He thinks that because, by giving this or that drug and producing this or that effect in a person (or because of the result of the practices of some of the strange cults he has investigated in various parts of the world), he has invalidated the Christian claim. He says, "I have seen everything that John Wesley and Jonathan Edwards used to produce."

The simple answer, of course, is that any experience with which we meet is bound to show itself through our brains and central nervous system. It is the same set of physical mechanisms which respond either to an experience of God or to the effects of taking drugs. All that Sargant has demonstrated is that some of the physical responses to two types of experience are common to both. There is nothing new about this. Sargant's argument virtually comes to this: because various cults, by this or that procedure, can give this or that kind of experience (which include some which took place during the Wesley revivals), then the nature of what happened in these eighteenth century revivals must be regarded as just the same.

In other words, he says that the experience tells you something about the cause behind it. I would reply that if, for example, we take a phrase which we sometimes use, that a man is "madly in love with a girl," then according to Sargant's reasoning, it does not mean that there is a special and particular object of the love, it is just a case of madness. Am I making the point clear? "Madly in love" according to Sargant, is a case of madness, because a man who is "madly in love" behaves like the man who is mad. There is a similar response. He jumps about, throws his hat into the air and smiles broadly at everyone. If we follow Sargant's reasoning, we must conclude that there is no special love for a particular charming person. He is just "mad"!

This is equally the reply to those who think that because of the phenomena produced by LSD they can explain away the experiences of religion and religion itself. To quote John Barker again, "Very little indeed is known about the neural physiology of the brain, or even (except in descriptions of effect) of the global action of neuropsychopharmacological agents." It is a mouthful, but it is a very profound statement! He also adds, "It now becomes clear that we cannot identify experiences induced by LSD with an entity known as religious experience defined by content alone." In other words, various drugs, or methods of working people up into a high pitch of tension in meetings of a cult, tell us nothing about the being of God.

The Christian case is not founded upon experience, it is based upon great objective and external facts. It is important to emphasize this for sometimes well meaning evangelicals have thrown away the key at this point. I remember on one occasion at a conference of ministers, there had been a considerable discussion and one minister got up and said, "I don't care what they say, nothing can ever touch my experience."

I had to say, "My dear friend, you have thrown away the key if you base the defense of the faith all on your experience."

Our faith is founded on the great objective truths and facts of history, on the fulfilment of prophecy and the fact of the church. Our experience certainly confirms these truths, but our faith does not depend on it. Today in these matters which we are here discussing, we may be more confident. As these people report the results of their use of their drugs they are simply demonstrating how ignorant we all still are concerning the fundamentals of neurophysiology and the workings of the brain. Their results do not touch our main position.

We can, therefore, reassure those who believe that it is sinful to take drugs which relate to brain function that, where clinical trial and proper use have shown them to be valuable, they should be received with thanksgiving. All things in nature and scientific knowledge are the gifts of God and should be used to his glory. We are "fearfully and wonderfully made." Many things that God in his love and kindness has provided for our needs exist all around us for their due use. To accept and use them makes no difference to our faith and salvation.

Conclusion

My final word is that we need to avoid all crazes and fashions. There is urgent need for the maintenance of the due balance which we find in Scripture. The apostle Paul instructs us to, "Prove all things; hold fast that which is good" (1 Thess. 5:21). The apostle John cautions that we should "try" or "test the spirits" (1 John 4:1). We need accurately to assess the need of each troubled soul who seeks our aid, diagnosing them in terms of the Scripture's view of man, of man in sin and of man "born again." The necessary aid is all there in the Bible.

It simply needs our careful study and wise application—with great patience—to given cases. "Who is sufficient for these things?"

Appendix

The Moral Law

A useful example of Dr. Lloyd-Jones' approach and teaching methods is provided below from notes taken by a member of a London discussion group.*

1. Introductory

The first necessity is to dismiss several of the more mistaken views which have grown around this subject. Especially it is necessary to be clear concerning the intention and status of the Law as given on Sinai (recorded in Exodus 20 and in the books of Moses, that is, the Hebrew *Torah*) and Christ's Sermon on the Mount, as recorded in Matthew 5:7.[1]

2. Misunderstandings

There have been four main misconceptions—

    (a) The Law of Sinai has been regarded as addressed only to

*From the introduction and summing up of a discussion on the relevance today of the moral law of the Old Testament held at the London Medical Study Group of the Christian Medical Fellowship on December 7, 1959.

Israel and as being obsolete in reference to other peoples to-day.

(b) On the contrary, the Sermon on the Mount, with its Beatitudes, has been taken as if it were applicable to the world at large. But our Lord addressed it to his disciples—the children of the kingdom of God.

(c) Others by a strange use of distinctions in biblical history based on different "dispensations" have *postponed* the real application of the Sermon to *a future completed* kingdom of God.

(d) But perhaps the most damaging misunderstanding of all is the liberal theologian's claim that he "holds to the *ethics* of the Sermon and of Christianity in general, but no longer accepts the doctrines." The point here is that, as the Bible presents the matter, the ethics plainly arise from the doctrine.

Then there are several other distortions of which the chief may be called:

3. False patronage

(a) Moses is often acclaimed (especially in a medical setting) as "the best medical officer of health, or community physician, the world has yet seen" and as having had a unique insight into the problems of public health. But as soon as one mentions Moses' God, the latter seems regarded as just some tribal deity.

(b) In a similar way, Jesus of Nazareth is applauded as "the wisest teacher" and the "greatest prophet" that the world has known. His sayings or "maxims" are an excellent source for telling quotes and apposite proverbs! But as soon as he talks of the purpose of his coming and the supreme aim of his life, that is quite another matter. They do not wish to go into doctrine.

This brings us to certain considerations which must be borne in mind. These are:

4. Two important distinctions

(a) God's Moral Law is of lasting and universal validity. It was already present for Adam and the patriarchs, who followed him. It will last on until the end of the human race. It remained in Adam after the fall as part of the defaced "image of God." Traces of the original Moral Law are still in man's heart and he has to come to terms with it unless he (as Paul says) "holds down the truth in unrighteousness" so that his conscience becomes "seared."

(b) *The Law in Sinai*, while initially addressed to Israel, embodies for all time something of the character of God and what (as Paul says) "is holy and just and good" for man. It codifies the essential principles of the Moral Law, of which the remains are in man's heart. ("The Law" is not just the Ten Commandments as found in Exodus 20, but its minor principles are also illustrated and applied throughout the five books of Moses.)

The crucial point in the history of the Moral Law comes when the New Testament (as the Book of the New Covenant) brings before us the important change which came about through the life, death and resurrection of Christ. He lived under the Law and died under the Law. As one result there came:

5. An official disuse of parts of the Law

(a) The *Political Law* of the Hebrews ceased with Israel's nationhood at the destruction of Jerusalem in A.D. 70.

(b) The *Ceremonial Law* of the Hebrews ceased when Christ had made "one sacrifice for sins for ever" and animal sacrifices were no longer required.

(c) But the *Moral Law* (as codified, for example, in the Ten Commandments) remained in force. Our Lord distinctly says that he did not come to destroy the Moral Law but to fulfil it, and to make it possible (under the New Covenant) for his disciples to keep it. Again, Paul reiterates that it is "holy, and just, and good" (Rom. 7:12).

Hence, it is important to be quite clear about the way in which the apostles saw the relation between the timeless universal Moral Law as codified under the Old Covenant and the Sermon on the Mount as given on the eve of the New Covenant.

6. The relevance of the Sermon on the Mount

(a) The leaders of Israel, the Pharisees and Sadducees, regarded their Law as something external to themselves to be obeyed, that is, a Code to be meticulously applied by a series of rule-of-thumb practices. The Sermon, on the other hand, comes in at a different angle and goes to the heart of the matter on each point. It is concerned rather with a disciple's *motives* and the *disposition* of his heart towards God and his neighbor. In the words of Jeremiah (Jer. 31:33), God says in reference to the New Covenant—"I will put my law in their inward parts, and write it in their hearts."

(b) When our Lord in the Sermon uses the emphatic "*but* I say unto you," he does not mean that he is abrogating the timeless Moral Law. He is rather emphasizing the fact that God is concerned with motives and disposition. "For man looketh on the outward appearance, but the Lord looketh on the heart" (1 Sam. 16:7).

(c) In effect our Lord goes back to the time when God's Moral Law was clearly written in the heart of man "as the image of God" and he is concerned to stress the new writing on the hearts of the children of God—with their new natures received from new birth in Christ.

(d) Again, it must be clearly seen that the "Second Table of the Law"—that is, the last six commandments dealing with duty to one's neighbor—was given in the context of the First Table, that is, of duty to God. Similarly, the second section of the Sermon dealing with love towards neighbors is on the basis of, "Thou shalt love the Lord thy God with all thy heart, and will all thy soul, and will all thy mind."

Neither the requirements of the Moral Law in the Commandments, or in the Sermon, should be separated from the Giver, and the basis on which they were given.

(e) In other words, the requirements of the Sermon on the Mount cannot be kept apart from what the New Testament has to say about regeneration of heart, purification of motive and a new dynamic provided by the gospel. Obedience requires as its corollary the inward presence and work of the Holy Spirit regenerating, purifying and enabling.

(f) It is clear (and many well disposed men of good will readily recognize this) that the results of the Second Table of the Law and its New Testament parallel in the Sermon on the Mount are very good for the community's general welfare. But New Testament ethics cannot be applied (in any detail) to mankind in general. For the Sermon was clearly addressed to disciples in the context of the teaching of the New Testament. Excellent as it is (and with all its potential for the good of mankind) both in theory and practice it is embedded in the basic teachings of the gospel.

The central problem, therefore, is concerning—

7. The universality of the Sermon

(a) Many members of the public, especially Jews, Roman Catholics and (to some extent) Muslims, will agree that the Second Table of Old Testament Law is for the good of society. Primitive societies may show also survivals of the Moral Law in their hearts. The Second Table of the Law, however—even though it is of universal validity and application—to become effective requires to be kept in its original setting of duty to God. The Second Table cannot be properly applied without obedience to God's claims in the First.

(b) How, then, can this matter be put to a non-Christian? A public figure recently said on television that he still held to the ethics of Christianity while sitting loose to its doctrines. But *can* he?

In the first instance, a man does not have a true view of self without seeing himself as God sees him. When he breaks down in trying to meet the Second Table's requirements he usually does not recognize the true source of his weakness and failure. The ultimately missing factor is a true recognition of God and an adequate dynamic in the light of the First Table.

(c) Emil Brunner in his *Divine Imperative* puts the matter like this: "Our grandfathers had the full Christian position, holding to both Tables of the Law and both parts of the Sermon. Their sons sought to hold on to the Second Table and its beneficient effects, whilst letting the First Table imperceptibly slip from them. The fathers thought that they could pass on the ethics without the doctrines, but now the grandsons have lost *both* the ethics and the doctrines."

(d) The Victorian evangelicals had one weakness which has accentuated these losses. While they believed what the Bible taught and desired to take proper action to overcome evil in all its forms, they made the mistake of tackling each evil separately. So, in the event, they organized temperance societies and then a separate society for every imaginable evil or need! But you cannot efficiently isolate each sin for national correction. Also, the strategy was ineffective because it tended to move them away from the all-essential inward motivation and spiritual dynamic with which the pioneers started. In contrast, the eighteenth and nineteenth century religious revivals went to the doctrinal heart of the matter. John Wesley told his followers to aim at the head of the serpent and the coils would look after themselves. When people and committees were deeply affected by a truly Christian conversion and inward renewal, both individual and public sins soon began to decline in power and extent. The central doctrine is the indispensable source of the dynamic of the ethics.

(e) Paul was very definite about this matter of the perpetual influence of the Moral Law in the hearts of men. He refers to "the law written in their hearts . . . accusing or else excusing" (Rom. 2:15), and goes on to explain that it was not only the Jews, but also the Gentiles, who had the Law in their hearts. We can point to its codification in the Second Table of the Law as that which men ought to accept and do. But from whence will they derive the adequate motivation and obey it? Life on this plane is portrayed in the Sermon on the Mount. It is here that our Lord's teaching becomes plain that to meet the requirements of the Sermon needs a new heart, a new motivation and a new dynamic. It arises out of "Thou shalt love the Lord thy God with all thy heart, and with all thy soul, and with all thy mind."

Then, there is the question of natural law and its relevance to man's responsibility and actions. This phrase needs to be carefully defined because the term is frequently used in more senses than one. Also, if applied out of its context, it is liable to cause more confusion.

8 The meaning of natural law

(a) In modern times the term natural law has most commonly been used to refer to the physical laws of nature. Utilitarianism, Darwinism and Marxism have attempted to evolve an ethic appropriate to these physical laws in the social sphere. But in older theology the term was used for the common denominator of ethics which were left to man after the fall. Augustine believed that the "image of God" had been so damaged that the residual awareness of God and awareness of moral duty were comparatively small, so that divine revelation and grace were needed before there could be a right use of reason and moral responsibility. The mediaeval church followed Thomas Aquinas, who used the term natural law in a special sense in which (based on an Aristotelian view of man) he regarded the damage to "the image of God" in man as having been considerably less than Augustine, and he affirmed that man was capable of the right use of his unaided reason and moral responsibility. Revelation and grace were supplementary and corrective of this.

(b) The Bible, and especially Romans 2 and Jude, *does* recognize a natural law to the extent that in fallen man there was still a surviving element of "the image of God," for example, in man's awareness of the divine being and the promptings of his conscience. Try as men may to overcome it, conscience still continues to protest against injustice and other wrongs until it becomes "seared" and silenced.

(c) The primeval law in man's heart is an elementary form of the Moral Law in so far as the latter enshrines what *in principle* God has set in man's heart. This is basic to Paul's argument in Romans 2. When showing "the new and living way" of the gospel he seeks to demonstrate the value and glory of the gospel for both Jew and Gentile. To do this he demonstrates that the Jew has the Law in a formulated code and the Gentile the Law in an unformulated form in his conscience. But both, in any case, continue to break it. Hence, the need for and the glory of the gospel.

(d) Lecturers on comparative religion constantly assert, because some elements of the Moral Law are found among primitive peoples, that these principles as formulated did not come through God to Moses in the written Law. They suggest rather that the Jews had a genius for religion and Moses as one of their major prophets simply refined what was common to primitive man into the Jewish Law. If we follow the Bible, however, we must claim that both forms of the Moral Law came from God, the residual inner principle in the hearts of primitive people and the codified Law on Sinai.

9. The Sermon and motivation

(a) It must be carefully noticed that Moral Law says, "Thou shalt do no murder." This must be kept technically separate in thought from the verb to "kill." People in this context continually keep talking of "killing," which—alas—is sometimes necessary in the course of maintaining law and order. The problems of pacificism and euthanasia, however, must be discussed in another context than that of murder, which is the point in the Law and the Sermon.

(b) This distinction is accompanied by others in the interpretation of the Sermon which primarily is concerned with *motives*. It asks whether you *hate* someone in your heart—for, if so, this is the *seed* of murder. Similarly throughout the Sermon, we must continually focus our attention on the motives illustrated and the context of what is being said. The rights and wrongs of some of the modern legal matters and the problems of medical ethics must be kept in their respective appropriate settings.

(c) The Pharisees and Sadducees were actually convinced that they were successfully keeping the Moral Law, and some were inclined to boast about this. Their interpretation of the Law was demonstrably wrong, as our Lord set out to prove. He asks: "Do any of you use such words as 'Raca' or 'You fool'? Do any of you know lust?" He then shows how these are breaches of the Law because they are really incipent hatred and adultery. These religious people had mechanized the Law into a system of rule-of-thumb habits and overlooked the motives. (Some pacifists, and other pressure groups who are careless interpreters of Scripture, tend to do the same sort of mechanizing of Scripture today.)

(d) The position is that all men are responsible before God to attempt to reach the first milestone. This includes both those who have the unformulated residual Moral Law in

183

their hearts, as well as those who have its codification in the Second Table of the Law of Sinai. Paul is quite definite in this assertion of those facts. But Christians, because of Table 1 of the Law—that is, the God whom they love and serve, and the gospel of the New Covenant into which they have now come—should hasten to apply themselves with zeal to the practice of the Sermon on the Mount—their motivation and dynamic is the love and service of God through the aid of the Holy Spirit.

Summary

The chief points to be kept in mind are:

1. The Sermon on the Mount can only be applied fully to the Christian, in light of his regeneration in Christ and his new motivation which arises from his love for God and his devotion to his service.

2. Many men, however, will be ready to consider the general provisions of Table 2 of the Law of Sinai, and also the general ethical aims and points of the Sermon. If these could be enforced, they are obviously very salutary for a community, and the lawgivers also would be interested.

3. But, it must be carefully shown that men cannot just have the ethics of the Sermon, without its doctrine, that is, without its roots in the love of God.

4. Today in the breakdown in law and order, and the undermining of general community life, even the advanced materialist politicians are afraid of the growing vacuum. They *may* perhaps be induced to see that the ideal for community ethics is a truly Christian society, based on the Law and the Sermon. At the same time, however, it must be made clear that the beneficient results are impossible to achieve without the control of Table 1 of the Law in which God declares—"Thou shalt have no other gods before me"; and without the basis of the ethics of the New Covenant as set out in the Sermon.

5 Today there is everywhere a widespread listlessness, loss

of interest and loss of nerve. For many students and other adolescents life has become meaningless. Morals—that is, the concept of Moral Law—cannot be suspended, as it were, in midair. It needs the rock-like foundation of faith in God on which to build the kind of life for which so many crave. All else ends in atrophy and disillusion.

Notes

Introduction

1. D. Martyn Lloyd-Jones, *Conversions: Psychological and Spiritual* (Inter-Varsity Press, 1959).

Chapter 2

1. Kathryn Kuhlman, *I Believe in Miracles* (Lakeland, 1968).
2. Kathryn Kuhlman, *God Can Do It Again* (Marshall, Morgan & Scott, 1969).
3. B. B. Warfield: *Miracles, Yesterday and Today* (Eerdmans, Michigan, 1953), first published as *Counterfeit Miracles* (Scribner, 1918).

Chapter 3

1. The editor of *The Practitioner* was present on this occasion.
2. McFarlane Burnett, *Genes, Dreams and Realities* (Penguin, 1973).
3. Ibid.

Chapter 4

1. Report of a conference arranged by associations concerned with the hospital service in Great Britain and Northern Ireland, May 14–15, 1968, in the Isle of Man. (Private circulation.)
2. Lord Todd: address to the BMA, Clinical Meeting, Cheltenham, October 24, 1968.

Chapter 5

1. See chapter 10, "Body, Mind and Spirit."

Chapter 6

1. It is here that so many modern Christians are inferior to the Reformers. The theology and ethical outlook of some is almost entirely confined to God's action in redemption, and they seem to imagine that they can contract out of God's ordinances as "God the Creator." Yet redemption is seen in its grandeur only in the context of the creation and the Moral Law.
2. Since this address was given there have been progressive nationwide changes which, the speaker observed later, would require modification of his remarks here.

Chapter 9

1. See chapter 10, "Body, Mind and Spirit."
2. Henry Miller, *Medicine and Society* (Oxford University Press, 1973).
3. Seymour Halleck, *The Politics of Therapy* (New York: Harper and Row, 1972).
4. William Sargant, *Battle for the Mind* (Heinemann, 1957).

Chapter 10

1. Frank Lake, *Clinical Theology* (Darton, Longman & Todd, 1981).
2. A fuller account of this case will be found in Dr. Martyn Lloyd-Jones, *Exposition of Romans 8:5–17* (Banner of Truth Trust, 1974).
3. Thomas Szasz, *The Manufacture of Madness* (Routledge and Kegan Paul, 1971)
4. Robert Peterson, *The Roaring Lion* (Overseas Missionary Fellowship, 1968).
5. Doreen Irvine, *From Witchcraft to Christ* (Concordia, 1973).
6. R. C. Zaehner, *Drugs, Mysticism and Make-Believe* (Collins, 1972).
7. John Bowker, *The Sense of God* (Clarenden Press, 1973).

Appendix

1. One of the most helpful of Dr. Lloyd-Jones' publications for medical practitioners has been *Studies in the Sermon on the Mount* (Inter-Varsity Press, 1976). It is worth its cost for the introduction and definitions alone.

Bibliography

Dr. Martyn Lloyd-Jones was primarily a preacher and wished to remain so. To safeguard his persuasive speaking gift and main strength, which was clarity of exposition and authority in the pulpit, he resisted numerous pressing invitations from admirers and publishers to write. This he regarded as a quite different gift, the use of which could easily spoil the particular ability of a preacher. Hence, it was not until the approach of his retirement that he found the time and inclination to make ready the manuscripts and to correct the proofs for the considerable number of volumes which eventually came to be completed. Earlier, however, through the industry of several members of his congregation and the increase of technical means for recording, tapes of some of the important series of addresses were produced. Several of these have proved very useful to members of the medical profession, especially:

1958 *Authority*, addresses from an International Conference, Canada, 1957 (Inter-Varsity Press).

1959 *Studies in the Sermon on the Mount* (Inter-Varsity Press). First published in two volumes and now one volume of 658 pages.

1959 *Conversions: Psychological and Spiritual* (Inter-Varsity Press). This is a booklet written in reply to William Sargant's *Battle for the Mind.*

1965 *Spiritual Depression: Its Causes and Cure* (Pickering & Inglis).

1970 *Daily Readings from the Works of Martyn Lloyd-Jones Selected by Frank Cumber* (Epworth).

1971 *Preaching and Preachers* (Hodder & Stoughton). Lectures in Westminster Theological Seminary.

1970–75 *Expositions of the Epistle to the Romans* (Banner of Truth Trust). Chapters 3:20–8:39 (eight volumes). The keys to the study are in Vol. I (3:20–4:25) and Vol. II (chapter 5).